THE
STAGECOACH
IN
NORTHERN CALIFORNIA

THE
STAGECOACH
IN
NORTHERN CALIFORNIA

ROUGH RIDES, GOLD CAMPS & DARING DRIVERS

CHERYL ANNE STAPP

Charleston London

THE
History
PRESS

Published by The History Press
Charleston, SC 29403
www.historypress.net

First published 2014

Manufactured in the United States

ISBN 978.1.62619.254.6

Library of Congress CIP data applied for.

For Murry

CONTENTS

CONTENTS

ACKNOWLEDGEMENTS

Researching the times and lives of the individuals who made the stagecoach an enduring icon of California's gold rush history has been fascinating, and I am indebted to the written accounts of observers who lived in the nineteenth century, as well as the works of modern historians. I wish to thank the dedicated professionals and other enthusiasts who helped me find a specific document or interesting story: the marvelous librarians at the California State Library, Sacramento, and staff members at the Placer County Archives, the Shasta County Historical Society and the Amador County Chamber of Commerce. Special thanks go to Dr. Kenneth Umbach for his invaluable assistance and to Allen Rountree, a wonderfully wise docent at the Sunnyvale Museum.

PART I

WESTERN STAGING BEGINS

California had no public transportation before 1849. Overland wayfarers rode their own, or borrowed, horses and mules. Families visited relatives in plodding oxen-powered *carretas*, simple carts with wheels hewn from solid slices of tree trunks.

Passersby who stopped for a night's rest at isolated ranches were entrusted to deliver letter mail to destinations along their expected routes. If no sojourner materialized, ranchers and town merchants pressed an employee into service as a mounted courier. When necessary or more expedient, private watercraft took small numbers of passengers over the rivers. For the most part—until their peace was shattered in the summer of 1846 by the Mexican-American War—residents of sparsely populated California, a half-neglected province of Mexico, lived their lives at a leisurely pace.

Everything changed with two near-simultaneous events in early 1848: gold was discovered in the Sierra Nevada foothills, and a week later the Treaty of Guadalupe Hildago that ended the Mexican-American War ceded California to the United States. The treaty was not announced until July, after it had been ratified by both governments. By then, however, upward of four thousand bedazzled gold prospectors from various Pacific Coast regions were working the streams and ravines. The following year, tens of thousands of gold seekers from all over the world swarmed into northern California by land and sea.

Before the stagecoach, those arriving by sea walked forty miles and more to the gold fields from inland river landings.

THE STAGECOACH IN NORTHERN CALIFORNIA

The volume of mail in the hulls of incoming ships increased a thousand fold, and lonely miners in isolated camps clamored for delivery of letters from loved ones back home. Successful prospectors needed reliable conveyance of their freshly mined gold to bankers' safes down in the valleys and coastal towns, which were suddenly teeming with individuals of diverse skills who had come to exploit ground-floor economic and political opportunities. Before the stagecoach tied them all together, the exchange of news and commerce between mining districts and far-apart settlements was confined to mule teams, lumbering wagons and just two navigable rivers.

Alexander Todd, a luckless but enterprising young miner, is generally credited with being the first to establish a mail and express service in 1849—when there was no official postal delivery provided—between the San Francisco post office and the mining camps. He went from camp to camp soliciting "subscribers," who gladly paid him one dollar apiece to list their names and an additional ounce of gold for each letter he brought them. He used surefooted pack mules and was so successful at delivering mail that miners and merchants alike asked him to carry their gold dust for deposit in San Francisco vaults. Todd purchased a rowboat to accommodate his increased cargoes, wending down the San Joaquin River and across San Francisco Bay. At the seaport, there were always men anxious to get to the mining districts, and Todd allowed passengers, charging each man a sixteen-dollar "tax" for the privilege of rowing his boat. The number of men he could take on any one trip was limited, and rowing upriver—especially in bad weather—usually wasn't fast.

Speed was the new imperative—for communication between sprouting civic centers and to transport shiploads of excited fortune-seekers who were in a hurry to reach the gold fields. Speed was the urgent need, but also welcome was the shelter from the elements that a stagecoach could provide. The iconic image of a rumbling Wells Fargo stagecoach drawn by six galloping horses has become the modern symbol of staging in the Old West, but Wells Fargo wasn't the first in gold-fevered California, and the company didn't own any stagecoaches until years after the gold rush ended.

Historians are divided in their opinions over who, between two primary candidates, established the first stage line in California: John Whisman or James E. Birch. Both started up in 1849 with borrowed, dilapidated equipment and fidgety horses; both charged a thirty-two-dollar fare. Whisman founded a fifty-mile stage service between San Francisco and San Jose. Birch founded stage transport from Sacramento to the gold-rich settlements of Coloma and Mormon Island in the Sierra foothills, ten miles shorter than Whisman's route but over steeper and rougher ground.

Crowds at the San Francisco Post Office in the 1850s, anxious for news from home. *Library of Congress, from a lithograph by William Endicott & Co.*

The claim for Whisman is based solely on the reminiscences of one of his drivers, Henry Ward. Ward stated that John Whisman was the first stage operator "in this part of California...in the fall of 1849"—without specifying the month. An advertisement in Sacramento's *Placer Times* confirms that James Birch was already in the staging business there before the end of July. Both are bested for first place by this June 28, 1849 advertisement in the *Weekly Alta California*:

> *MAURISON & COMPANY'S EXPRESS AND MAIL LINE. The undersigned would respectfully inform the public that they have established a line of Stages between Stockton and the Stanislaus Mines, for the accommodation of passengers and baggage. A stage will leave Stockton every other day for the mines, at 4 o'clock, A.M., and arrive at the other end of the route in 12 hours. Returning, a Stage will leave the mines at the same hour on the intermediate days, and arrive at Stockton at 4 o'clock, P.M.*

Unlike Alexander Todd, Maurison was not an authorized mail carrier and likely operated his business as the sole driver of an open wagon for only a short time before he partnered in the new enterprise Ackley & Maurison, running stages out of San Jose. Perhaps disheartened by the entry of these rivals, John Whisman sold out in 1850 to Warren F. Hall and Jared B. Crandall, two Yankees who had operated a stage line from Vera Cruz to Mexico City and who had both the expertise and the capital to ensure success. In the Sacramento Valley, James Birch—undisputedly the first to service the northern gold country—flourished. Within five years of his humble beginnings, Birch established the California Stage Company—the largest stage line in the nation.

THE STAGECOACH: GLAMOUR AND UTILITY

The word "stage" had two applications. When speaking of a vehicle, a stage was any coach, wagon or sleigh used to haul passengers and baggage for staging purposes. "Stage wagon," or "mud wagon," was distinct in its meaning from "stagecoach" or "coach." In its original and stricter meaning, a stage was a section of road between relays of animals along a given route, commonly called a "line" or a "drive." Stations were either "home stations" or "swing stations." Generally, a station master and his family resided at a home station and provided meals to travelers. Swing stations were for purposes of relay only.

There were different styles of staging vehicles, a fact now all but forgotten, as the image of the magnificent Concord coach—glorified in paintings, exhibits and big-screen westerns—has mostly obliterated general awareness of the less glamorous mud wagons, celerity wagons and other conveyances.

The direct ancestor of the nineteenth-century American stagecoach was the eighteenth-century English road wagon, modified by colonial artisans for New World roads in a quadrangular design commonly called a stage waggon (with two *g*'s). Eventually, developing technology placed springs beneath the passenger seats, and the vehicle bodies were suspended on thoroughbraces—layered, heavy leather straps that allowed the coach to rock and sway in a cradle-like motion to spare the horses from the shocks of the road. About 1820, the body profile of the vehicle evolved into an oval-shape with a rounded top, and the term "stagecoach" came into common usage. The Albany coach, manufactured in Albany, New York, achieved wide favor until it was eclipsed by the Troy coach, a popular style manufactured in the neighboring city of Troy. In the late 1820s, skilled wheelwright Lewis Downing of Concord, New Hampshire, and experienced chaise builder J.

A beautifully restored 1860s Concord stagecoach. *Photo by author.*

Stephens Abbot (originally from Maine) began designing and manufacturing a masterpiece of construction that had no equal: the Concord stagecoach.

The partners, each a superb craftsman, used only the finest seasoned ash and white oak for the body and wheels, the prime sections of a dozen ox hides per vehicle for the thoroughbrace suspension and other leather items, and hand-forged Norway iron for precision-fitted tires and railing around the roof to help secure piled luggage. Each piece of wood in the body was steamed into pliability and then hand-molded into precise curves. Wheel spokes were shaped by hand to the exact measurement and weight of the other spokes in the same wheel. The rear luggage boot was lined in weatherproof canvas and covered by oiled black leather. Another, smaller boot in front supported the high driver's bench, serving as a footrest and additional baggage space. This construct, with room for two passengers next to the driver, was commonly called "the box." Three more could sit on top behind the driver's bench. A door on each side had a glazed window (later eliminated in coaches for western delivery) and open windows on both sides of the door. Heavy leather curtains rolled down and latched over these to shield travelers from inclement weather. A footbrake at the driver's right activated a rear-wheel clamping mechanism.

THE STAGECOACH IN NORTHERN CALIFORNIA

Artist's sketch of M.P. Henderson & Company's carriage factory in Stockton. *Author's collection.*

The finished product was a durable vehicle that weighed 2,500 pounds empty. Special features included lanterns attached at the front.

Inside, the coach was upholstered in padded leather and damask and typically held six passengers, or nine with the addition of a center bench. The crowning touch was the paint job: two hand-rubbed coats finished with two or more coats of varnish and polished to a gleam. Exquisite hand-painted miniature landscapes graced the doors. The Concord was the envy of every stage operator who couldn't afford one.

Priced from $1,200 to $1,500 at the factory (approximately $240,000 to $300,000 or more in the late twentieth century), the purchase of Concord coaches, plus the cost of transporting them from New Hampshire to California by ship around Cape Horn, was a significant investment. Still, this cost was accepted by the discerning despite the fact that before the end of the 1850s, several California coach makers had their products on the market, among them Raish & Bellnap in Marysville, Young & Pike's Carriage Manufactory in Sacramento and H. Casebolt & Company in San Francisco, the latter enjoying a reputation for producing high-quality vehicles.

In September 1869, Milton Henderson, a carriage woodworker from Maine, and E.G. Clark, a blacksmith, established a carriage manufactory in Stockton that was soon renowned for its superior products. Founded as Henderson & Clark, the firm became M.P. Henderson & Company after Clark's retirement. The company was so successful that in 1879, Henderson purchased property at the corner of Main and American Streets, where he erected a substantial three-story brick factory-and-showroom building, augmented later by adjoining lots with wooden structures and drying yards. Stagecoaches, drays, specialty wagons and hearses were made to order for customers in all parts of the Pacific Coast, the Southwest and Hawaii. Milton Henderson retired in 1885 and died in his Stockton home in 1907. His son Orrin continued as M.P. Henderson & Son in the manufacture of coaches and wagons that were acclaimed for their excellence and durability.

LESSER COACHES AND OTHER CONVEYANCES

Cheers and applause greeted the first Concord coach to arrive in California via clipper ship as it paraded around San Francisco's city plaza in June 1850. More followed. Admirable as it was, however, the Concord performed best in dry weather on the better roads—and northern

A typical mud wagon. *Author's collection.*

California was fairly riddled with rough uphill trails that became muddy quagmires in winter.

Used more often than full-bodied coaches, mud wagons—as their name suggests—were built to travel over more rugged roads in winter rainstorms without becoming mired. Square-bodied, homely conveyances with canvas roofs, they were open at the sides above flat wooden panels. To protect passengers against rain or snow, heavy outside canvas curtains could be rolled down from the top and fastened. Mud wagons weighed from 800 pounds for a common nine-passenger model to 1,200 pounds for one that seated fourteen and cost about one-third the price of a premier coach. Tough and durable, their lower center of gravity was good for the type of mountain roads that serviced mining camps. Baggage was stored in the single rear boot or piled inside with the passengers. Manufactured by Abbot-Downing and others, mud wagons had the same type of thoroughbrace suspension as the larger Concord coaches.

Celerity wagons, manufactured by coach works in New York and New Hampshire, had light, maneuverable frames that allowed for fast travel over sandy ground. Similar to mud wagons in function and appearance, they were also designed for passenger travel at night. The backs of the seats let down to form a bed the length of the vehicle; if the stage was full, passengers had to take turns sleeping.

A wide range of public and personal conveyances soon became available in California, some differentiated only by their advertised functional uses or manufacturer-designated model numbers. "Omnibus" was a nineteenth-century term for what today is simply called a bus. Long and rectangular in shape, the omnibus ferried multiple passengers around city streets. It was seldom used as a stage. A "hack" was a two-wheeled vehicle for hire, a nineteenth-century taxi. Buggies and somewhat grander carriages were one- or two-horse, private-use vehicles.

STAGE TEAMS AND TRADITIONS

Little information exists to document how most pioneer stage lines acquired their teams. The qualities for a good stage horse included strength, endurance and speed, and it's possible that thousands of California horses in 1849 met those qualifications. But few—if any—had ever pulled a stagecoach; certainly not the swift and agile saddle horses belonging to the huge cattle ranches established in the Spanish and Mexican periods. Since the mid-1840s, American settlers had driven small herds of domesticated horses across the prairies—but these animals, if young and healthy, commanded premium prices that escalated into the triple digits as the gold rush population swelled. Most of the readily available stock was the wild descendants of horses brought by various expeditions from Mexico in decades past and allowed to roam freely over vast ranchlands as their numbers increased. These creatures presented other complications: extra time invested in breaking them to the bare fundamentals of acceptable equine behavior, and even then, the greater risk that half-wild mustangs might bolt and topple a stage. The consequences were not only damage and injury to coach and passengers but also the potential loss of coveted government mail contracts by stagemen who failed to demonstrate the safety of their operations.

Just as important as equipment and teams were the precedents and traditions set on the East Coast long before staging began in the West. Congressional legislation enacted in 1785 allowed stagecoaches to carry the U.S. mail on established, regularly scheduled routes that extended farther than a town or two. Eastern express services transported financial documents and other valuables by stagecoach. Stage lines carried newspapers as well, thus disseminating a broader scope of news and information. Until railroads and the telegraph became common in the East after 1840, the stagecoach was the principal mode of communication between towns and villages and therefore the primary encouragement to trade between them. These benefits, traditions and practices continued in California, where stage service to the mines facilitated the flow of the prodigious amounts of gold that transformed a sleepy backwater region into a major trade and industrial state.

PART II

MEN OF VISION

James E. Birch: The California Stage Company

Twenty-one-year-old James Birch appeared one morning in 1849 on Sacramento's waterfront in a rented ranch wagon, shouting, "All aboard! All aboard for Mormon Island and Sutter's Mill!"

Sutter's lumber mill was at Coloma, the site of James Marshall's stunning gold discovery. Mormon Island was another famous locale, a gold-rich gravel bar downstream from Coloma on the American River. His wagon was full that day, and every day thereafter, at thirty-two dollars per passenger—in pre–gold rush days, a month's wages for an unskilled laborer. Birch used his profits to invest in needed road improvements and better teams and equipment.

Other than the fact that James Birch was born in South Carolina on November 30, 1827, nothing is known of his life until the mid-1840s, when Otis Kelton, a stable owner in Providence, Rhode Island, hired him as a stage driver. Jim fell in love with his employer's half-sister, Julia Chace, and pretty Julia dreamed of one day living in a beautiful, well-staffed mansion in her hometown of Swansea, Massachusetts. In early December 1848, when President James Polk confirmed feverish rumors that high-quality, extensive gold deposits existed in California's foothills, Jim Birch saw an opportunity to make his sweetheart's dreams come true.

However, December was the wrong season for land travel across the continent. Within a fortnight of this electrifying announcement, hundreds of Atlantic Coast residents scrambled aboard westbound vessels. Ships

Left: James E. Birch. *Courtesy California State Library, Sacramento.*

Below: James Birch's September 1849 advertisements in the *Sacramento Daily Union. Author's collection.*

For the Mines.

Birch's Express Line to Sutter's Mills, at Coloma, by way of Mormon Island, Leaves S. Brannan's store, Sacramento City, every morning at 7 o'clock. Returning will leave the St. Louis Exchange, at the Mills, every morning at 6 1-2 o'clock, (Sundays excepted.) Passengers can leave Sacramento City for Mormon Island (which is one mile from the North Fork) in the morning and return the same day, stopping one hour at the Island.. All business entrusted to the Proprietor of this Line will be promptly attended to. Seats may be secured and farther information obtained by applying at the Stage Office, Front street, Sacramento City.

JAMES BIRCH, Proprietor.

Sacramento City. Sept. 1, 1849.   18 tf

leaving New York reached Chagres in about thirteen days, and from there, passengers could make their way by various means across the hazardous fifty-mile isthmus to the port at Panama City, where they hoped to board a San Francisco–bound vessel coming north from around Cape Horn. The steamer *Crescent City* left New York on December 23, 1848; among its passengers were one Jas. Birch and a J. Davenport. This ship encountered problems en route, so how long it took its passengers to arrive at Chagres, reach Panama City and then sail north is unknown, but Birch and Davenport together established a stage service in Sacramento in July 1849.

On July 21, 1849, Sacramento's weekly *Placer Times* noted, "The new line of stages between this city and the Mill is in the full tide of successful operation. The gentlemanly and obliging proprietors deserve all the patronage they are receiving." A month later, on August 18, 1849, the same newspaper printed the following announcement:

> Dissolution. *The copartnership* [sic] *heretofore existing under the firm of Birch & Davenport, is this day dissolved by mutual consent. The Stage Business will be continued as heretofore by the subscriber.* JAMES BIRCH. *Sacramento City August 1ˢᵗ, 1849.*

Birch's September advertisements made it clear that he now had stages leaving Sacramento for the mines and *returning* every day, and he also secured a contract to carry the U.S. mail weekly from Sacramento to Coloma for a one-year term.

The winter floods of 1849–50 inundated Sacramento up to a mile east of the city, completely cutting off access to and from the mines. When the weather cleared in March, Birch advertised resumption of service to Mormon Island and Coloma with an added amenity—ongoing from that date—that was indicative of his promotional and public relations talents: passengers who purchased advance tickets at the office would be picked up at any hotel in the city. Two months later, he announced, "New Stage Arrangements for All the Northern Mines—Through by Daylight," listing extended stage service to mining communities "on the direct route to the North, South, and Middle Forks of the American River" that included Pilot Hill, Georgetown, Hangtown (Placerville) and other, now nonexistent communities. Jim Birch was still driving some of the routes himself and was complimented for his driving skills by the *Placer Times* editor, who went for an hour's "experimental ride."

Birch's shortened run times and the arrival of his "real" stagecoach (not a Concord) in the spring of 1850 caused a mild sensation. "Quick

Time," praised the *Placer Times* on April 22. "One of [Mr. Birch's stages] arrived here [from Coloma] on Saturday in seven hours…the usual time is eight hours. The splendid new coach which has attracted so much attention goes on in a day or two." With his mail contract due to expire on September 30, he sold his Sacramento–Coloma stage route interests to his drivers William Cole Jr. and Anson Briggs and moved on to larger markets, where he rightly expected that government mail contracts would be more lucrative.

On February 18, 1851, the *Sacramento Transcript* published a near eulogy:

> *NEW LINE OF STAGES.—Mr. James Birch, extensively known in this vicinity, has established a line of stages between Nicolaus and Marysville, in connection with the steamer* Gov. Dana. *He has fifty of the finest horses and the best coaches in California, and the way he puts through his passengers is a caution to slow teams. He has an abundance of passengers, as the* Gov. Dana *has carried one hundred passengers daily for the last two weeks. Mr. Birch, we believe, is the first man that established a stage line in this country. He is endowed with great perseverance and integrity, and if any person deserves success, it is James Birch. Passengers by this line can reach Marysville from this city in seven hours.*

The new arrangement between Nicolaus and Marysville was a preliminary move to a bigger undertaking: a stage service between Sacramento and Nevada City. In April 1851, Birch announced his new Telegraph Line: "Through in 11 Hours…Nevada City, Grass Valley, Rough and Ready, Johnson's Ranch, Marysville, Nicolaus and Sacramento City Daily Line of Stages…Passengers from Marysville can take the Stage at Nicolaus for Nevada City every day at half past 10 o'clock." On its first trip, the Telegraph Line made it through its stated schedule in a remarkable ten hours and twenty minutes.

The southern mines were also prosperous, and Birch didn't overlook their base town. On May 3, 1851, he established his Tri-Weekly Line of stages between Sacramento and Stockton, upgrading the service to a daily run shortly thereafter. At the end of May, Birch again displayed his flair for marketing by running four stages from Sacramento to the crowd-drawing horse races five miles east at Brighton for three days beginning on May 21. These "special accommodation" stages left every half hour from three hotels. By this time, dozens of other lines were operating in all of the major gold rush towns and most of the larger camps—although none, as yet, was as

A stagecoach entering Grass Valley's Mill Street. *Library of Congress, Lawrence & Houseworth Collection.*

successful as James E. Birch, whose solid character and skillful management had brought him material financial rewards.

In late October 1851, he sold out. The buyers of his Sacramento–Stockton stage service are unknown; James Haworth and E.C. Smith purchased the Telegraph Line. In early December, Birch returned east and built a mansion in Swansea, Massachusetts, for Julia Chace. They were married there on September 14, 1852.

Sometime in 1852–53, Frank Shaw Stevens took up residence in Sacramento and founded a stage service as F.S. Stevens & Company's Daily Express and Accommodation Lines between there and Placerville. Legend is the source of his pre-1849 friendship with James Birch—as is the undocumented, yet oft repeated, lore that Frank invested in a Sacramento hotel in 1850 and later founded the Pioneer Stage Line. But based on later events, the two obviously formed a close and lasting bond during the period when Frank was simultaneously operating his Sacramento–Placerville line and partnering with H.R. Covey in livery stables—first on Fourth Street and later at a larger facility on Third Street, as the *Sacramento Daily Union* informed its readers on September 19, 1853:

> *TO EQUESTRIANS—Frank Stevens, well known to our citizens as a capital connoisseur in horse flesh, has taken the commodious stables recently occupied by D. McDowell, on Third Street, near I. To those of our readers who are desirous of a "tip-top turn out," the carriages and steeds of Frank will give ample satisfaction, while his saddle nags are not surpassed by any horse flesh this side of the Rocky Mountains. We can cordially recommend the stock of this stable to those whose business avocations or schemes of pleasure require such property as is now in the possession of the accommodating Frank.*

Meanwhile, in March 1853 Birch returned to California, where he was hailed in the press as "The pioneer and founder of the present [staging] establishment...[who] could not resist the attractions of the country, and has purchased the Nevada Lines at $40,000 cash," referring to Birch's repurchase of his Telegraph Line. What he saw when he returned, however, was discomforting. During his sixteen months' absence, increased competition and the resultant forced lowering of fares had eroded stage owners' profits, although coaches were always crowded, and average speed on all the routes was ten miles per hour. Birch spoke with other stagemen from San Francisco, Marysville, Stockton and Sacramento, convincing them that all would be better off if they pooled their resources; more than 80 percent agreed. Arrangements for a joint stock association (later incorporated when a change in California laws permitted this form of business ownership), with headquarters in Sacramento, were completed in December.

On January 1, 1854, the California Stage Company, with $1 million in capital stock, commenced operations from the prestigious Orleans Hotel with James E. Birch and Frank Shaw Stevens as its president and vice-president. The trustees were Birch, Stevens, James Haworth (who had purchased Birch's Telegraph Line and resold it to him), O.N. Morse (who later bought the Covey & Stevens livery stable), Warren F. Hall of Hall & Crandall Stage Lines and four others. The California Stage Company was to become the largest and richest staging firm in America in the mid-nineteenth century.

Within three months, the organization was running so smoothly that Birch decided to go east for a time, both to visit his family and to place bids with the United States Post Office Contracts Department in Washington, D.C., which had announced that it would receive proposals for carrying the

Today a museum, the Elk Grove House, built in 1850, was a popular stage stop on the old road from Sacramento to Monterey. *Courtesy Elk Grove Historical Society.*

mail inside California for a four-year period beginning in July 1854. Birch was back by September, when he announced the company's first of many stock dividends.

While he was away, the *Sacramento Daily Union*, on June 3, 1854, published its review of the company's first six months, excerpted as follows:

> *STAGING—The entire stage travel to and from this city is now effected through the several lines of the California Stage Company. Fifty thousand dollars worth of property has been purchased…Their stock consists of over nine hundred head of horses…over one hundred coaches, besides a large number of feed-wagons, buggies, &c. The several lines give employment to over one hundred and fifty persons. There are now eleven lines radiating from this city, and daily traversed…in the aggregate, a distance of 1,470 miles every twenty-four hours.*

The routes identified included Sonora, Nevada City, Rough and Ready, Ophir and Auburn, Georgetown, Coloma, Placerville, Drytown, Jackson,

Rattlesnake Bar, Marysville and Placerville. Later in the year, the company added two routes to Shasta and a new policy: all passengers would be called for at their residences. In December, it pushed southward to Los Angeles, a venture later withdrawn.

A monopoly in certain areas, the California Stage Company was nonetheless praised. "This company is the first monopoly that we ever met with that succeeded in securing a general and warm popularity," the *Marysville Herald* enthused. "The cause undoubtedly is that...the officers of the company are all sensible and public spirited men...reflected in the courtesy and energy of Messrs. Birch [and his employees]." In early February 1855, Jim Birch again demonstrated his well-known gentlemanly character. Unasked, he generously donated coaches to the Sacramento Pioneer Association "in sufficient number" for the funeral cortege of one of its members.

But by now, Birch was pursuing an even larger challenge: a transcontinental stage service to carry mail and passengers on a regular schedule. To devote his full attention to this issue, he withdrew from all active participation in the California Stage Company while remaining its majority stockholder. James Haworth succeeded him as president.

In mid-February, Birch departed for his home in Swansea, where he remained for two years. In 1856, Jim and Julia had a baby boy, whom they named Frank Stevens Birch in honor of Jim's friend and California Stage Company vice-president Frank Shaw Stevens. Jim enjoyed an active social life with his wife but also devoted considerable time working with members of Congress who were influential in postal affairs. A major obstacle was the increasingly bitter division in the nation's capital between North and South interests. Both factions realized that any overland mail service would likely be followed eventually by a railroad along the same route—and each desired to control communications with the Pacific Coast.

Finally, on March 3, 1857, Congress passed a bill authorizing the postmaster general to contract for delivery of the entire U.S. letter mail overland to San Francisco in such a manner that included suitable means of conveying passengers. Birch and other stagemen submitted bids for what soon became known as "the great overland mail contract," and general expectations were that the mail would be carried over a central route—until Postmaster General Aaron Brown, a native of Tennessee, insisted that a road running through the South be used. President Buchanan abruptly put an end to the contest by directing Brown to award the six-year contract to Buchanan's long-standing personal friend, experienced stageman and American Express magnate John Butterfield, whose proposed route ran southwest from St. Louis; crossed Texas, New Mexico and Arizona to Los Angeles; and then swung north through the San Joaquin Valley to San Francisco. The famous Butterfield Overland Mail commenced in September 1858.

Earlier, Postmaster Aaron Brown had persuaded Jim Birch to accept a four-year contract to carry mail between San Antonio, Texas, and San Diego, California, to begin on July 1, 1857. Still hoping to secure the major award, Birch nonetheless turned his attention to the matter at hand: the first overland mail and passenger facility to the Pacific Coast, a distance of 1,475 miles over deserts and mountains. He at once hired Isaiah Woods, a thoroughly experienced stage-line operator, as superintendent. Woods had already stocked this route and was running mule-driven stages over it (later dubbed the "Jackass Mail" by enthusiastic San Diegans) when Birch reached California by steamer in the first week of August to meet with the officers and directors of the California Stage Company.

His business concluded, Birch was aboard the palatial side-wheeler *Central America* when it left the Panamanian Atlantic port of Colón on September 3. Six days later, the ship, laden with ten tons of California gold, was caught in a hurricane off the coast of the Carolinas that shredded its sails and damaged the boiler. A passing brig rescued 153 women and children, but despite heroic efforts by its crew and passengers, the *Central America* was swept farther out to sea, where it sank on September 12, 1857, four hundred miles off Cape Hatteras. Roughly 425 people were still on board when the ship went down, including James Birch. He was twenty-nine.

Six months later, Julia Chace Birch, as administratrix of her husband's estate, journeyed to Sacramento. Frank Shaw Stevens was there, offering his aid to the widow. They were married in Sacramento on July 24, 1858; soon thereafter, a probate court action named Stevens as the sole administrator. The couple returned together to Swansea to live in the Birch mansion and raise young Frank Stevens Birch. Frank Shaw Stevens continued as vice-president and director of the California Stage Company.

Competently steered by its president James Haworth, the California Stage Company grew and prospered, selling less profitable routes to initiate new ones in Monterey and elsewhere, in due time wheeling east over the formidable Sierra into Nevada and north into Oregon. Eight years after the death of James Birch, the company had 1,250 horses pulling stages over an aggregate 1,100 miles. With letters and the telegraph the only long-distance communication available, the sheer size of the geographically diverse staging empire made it more and more unwieldy to manage according to the company's high standards—and the eastbound tracks of the Central Pacific Railroad were resolutely heading toward the 2,400-foot elevation at Colfax. That same year, the company's mail contract from Sacramento to Portland expired, and it was unable to obtain a renewal on satisfactory terms. For these and probably other reasons, the directors of the California Stage Company decided to sell out. They did so quietly, selling their lines, teams and most of their equipment to various undisclosed individuals by September 1865. James Haworth had resigned as president in May. His replacement, a company director and Sacramento operations superintendent A.G. Richardson, finalized arrangements with buyers, agents and suppliers. In January 1866, Richardson advertised the sale of twenty-five "thoroughly repaired" Concord coaches and other assorted wagons, harness and tools to be closed out at public auction if still unsold after four months.

The previous October, the *Sacramento Daily Union* had learned of two major buyers:

> *We are informed that a number of capitalists of San Francisco, headed by Louis McLane, have purchased the stock of the company and taken the contract for the Oregon route. Last month the company sold their Virginia [City] line to the Pioneer Stage Company, and since, they have been closing out their various branch lines...As soon as they can wind up their affairs they will probably disincorporate and be numbered among the things that were.*

The Pioneer Stage Company had once been owned by Jared Crandall. Louis McLane, who held private interests in myriad California enterprises, was also the West Coast general agent for Wells Fargo & Company.

JARED CRANDALL: HALL & CRANDALL, THE PIONEER STAGE COMPANY AND THE PLACERVILLE ROAD

Residents of the small settlements along the fifty-mile road between San Francisco and San Jose gaped at the hard-driving, flat-out stagecoach race speeding past them, until the driver of the Hall & Crandall coach and the lone passenger sitting beside him waved their hats and shouted out glorious news: "California is admitted to the Union!" Wild cheering erupted as the vehicles flew past with their teams nearly neck and neck, cheers that did not quite drown out the din of thundering hooves and clattering wheels.

It was October 19, 1850. The previous morning, the steamship *Oregon*, gaily decorated from stem to stern and taffrail to maintop, had entered San Francisco Harbor with its guns cannonading, bearing the official announcement that California had been admitted to the Union on September 9. The wild race between rival stagelines Hall & Crandall and Ackley & Maurison was typical of their ongoing intense competition, and each was determined to be the first to deliver the news to the state capital at San Jose. Jared Crandall himself drove for the occasion, and the man seated next to him was Peter Burnett, California's recently elected first civil governor. Crandall won by minutes.

Jared Crandall. *Author's collection.*

In his *Recollections of an Old Pioneer*, written years later, Peter Burnett remembered the momentous event, describing Crandall as "one of the celebrated stagemen of California, like Foss and Monk. He was a most excellent man, and a cool, kind, but determined and skillful driver." Burnett might have said, as others did, that J.B. Crandall was "a prince of drivers."

Jared B. Crandall was born in Massachusetts about 1812. All that is known of his early staging career or personal life is that his wife was the former Mary Ann Moody, born in Vermont in 1814, and that two of their sons were born in Georgia in the early 1840s. Almost certainly, Crandall—as others did—went there to continue practicing a livelihood in staging; by 1840, the stagecoach days in New England were in decline, having been steadily displaced by the railroad's increasing miles of track. In Mexico, Don Jose Saratuso received a government contract to deliver the mail. Saratuso purchased American equipment and recruited American stage owners and drivers, offering premium wages and the payment of all expenses. Jared Crandall and brothers Warren and William Hall were among those who accepted this opportunity, and together the three operated a successful mail-delivery stage run between Vera Cruz and Mexico City.

News of the fabulous gold discovery in California reached Mexico and South America in the spring of 1848. Thousands of excited men departed immediately. At this early date, surface gold deposits were plentiful, and many were successful, but word filtered back that the total absence of public transportation in California severely hampered travel from seaport to inland mining districts, between rising new commercial centers and the geographically expanding mining camps. It was a chance to resurrect the former New England glory of the stagecoach that Crandall and the Hall brothers couldn't resist. As soon as practicable, the partners settled their business interests in Mexico, pooled their resources and headed north, where they organized as Hall & Crandall.

Meanwhile, John Whisman's San Francisco–San Jose operation was floundering due to bad winter weather, Whisman's ineffective management and the appearance of stage operators Ackley & Maurison in April 1850, rivals for the same route who undercut Whisman's fares. In the early spring of 1850, Hall & Crandall purchased Whisman's business, hired some of his drivers and began improving the stock and establishing stations along the route, building a first-class operation that would be eligible to receive a mail contract.

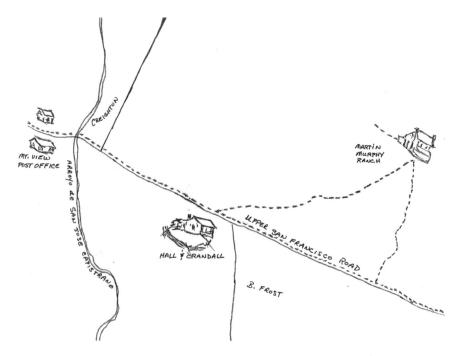

A section of a land survey map in Santa Clara County, 1850s. Upper San Francisco Road was part of the El Camino Real. *Drawing by artist Bob Shumate.*

According to reminiscences penned by driver Henry Ward, coach-trained horses were scarce, but there were thousands of wild mustangs in southern California, costing as little as six dollars a head. Wanting only the best stock—six-year-old mares weighing 1,100 pounds—and pressed for time, the partners contracted with Don Juan Forster (Englishman John Forster, brother-in-law of California's former Mexican governor Pío Pico and owner of two enormous ranches near San Diego and Los Angeles) for five hundred wild mares and fourteen stallions at twenty dollars per head. The stock was delivered at Los Angeles. In twenty days, the herd was on Hall & Crandall's ranch near modern Mountain View in Santa Clara County, where the arduous process of breaking them to harness began. Later in the year, they bought some eastern horses and thoroughbrace-suspension mud wagons that were driven across the plains by pioneer William Beeks, who retained enough stock and equipment to establish his own stage line between Sacramento and Nevada City in October 1850.

Hall & Crandall contracted with Richard Berford's respected Berford & Company Express (which served the coastal communities) to carry Berford's express and letter packets and also employed Berford & Company as its staging agents, but operated as a separate entity under its own name. While Beeks's Sacramento-based line posed no threat, Ackley & Maurison presented stiff competition—so the partners deliberately matched Ackley & Maurison's departure times from each end of the San Francisco–San Jose run and reduced their rates. In April 1851, Hall & Crandall received a four-year contract to carry the U.S. mail on this route three times a week, for $6,000 per year—this in addition to passenger tickets that were in high demand. Warren Hall went to New Hampshire to order Concord coaches from Abbot-Downing that were specially modified for California roads.

In July 1851, the partners announced an additional route from San Jose to Monterey, passing through Gilroy, and in August, a further reduction of their fares finally forced Ackley & Maurison out of business. The stagemen began offering in-city services by operating an hourly omnibus between San Francisco's city plaza and the Mission Delores and entering into agreements with other concerns that featured Hall & Crandall's name in their own publicity. The steamer *Jenny Lind*, which sailed between San Francisco's Long Wharf and Alviso, advertised that its schedule permitted passengers to connect with Hall & Crandall stages for San Jose. The following are other examples of these joint-interest marketing efforts:

THE STAGECOACH IN NORTHERN CALIFORNIA

MANSION HOUSE, San Jose—The enterprising mail contractors, Messrs. Hall & Crandall, to accommodate the traveling public, have furnished their Lines with the finest Concord coaches, and reduced the fare to $10 from this place to San Francisco; and leave the Mansion House daily at 7 o'clock A.M., and arrive at 3 o'clock P.M. in time to connect with the up-river boats. The same Line leaves for Monterey three times a week. Fare through from Monterey to San Francisco $25.
—Daily Alta California, *August 6, 1851*

WELCH'S—Having taken charge of the Hotel recently erected on the Pulgas Ranch, San Jose road...I respectfully solicit the patronage of the public. Families can be accommodated with board and private apartments. Carriages and saddle horses for hire. Stage passengers from and to San Jose to breakfast and dine. Hall & Crandall will dispatch a conveyance from San Francisco every Saturday at 12 o'clock, arriving in time for dinner at 6 o'clock. Returning, leave Monday morning at 6 o'clock and arriving at 12, thus affording an opportunity of visiting the country without loss of time. A. WELCH.
—Daily Alta California, *June 9, 1852*

A TRIP—ONE OF HALL & CRANDALL'S splendid coaches will leave the office of Bereford & Company at 12 o'clock for Steinberger's Hotel, on the San Jose road. This stage is put on the above mentioned route for the accommodation of gentlemen who may have a desire to spend a few hours away from the dust and turmoil of our busy streets. We understand that Messrs. H. & C. think of continuing this 12 o'clock arrangement, should sufficient encouragement be given. The stage will leave the hotel at 6 A.M. to return, and the passengers will arrive in San Francisco at 10 A.M.
—Daily Alta California, *June 12, 1852*

Profitable as they were on the coast, however, the partners were not immune to perceived greater golden opportunities in the interior. By 1852, Shasta City was a thriving, important commercial district both for its own gold-mining wealth and as a center for outlying camps. While still maintaining their San Francisco–San Jose lines, the Hall brothers and Jared Crandall simultaneously established daily stages from Colusa to Shasta and another from Marysville to Shasta in May 1852 (Redding did not exist at that time). The Marysville–Shasta line was a certified mail route with a southern terminus at Sacramento; both routes ran through Tehama City. The *Daily Alta California* editorialized as follows on June 7, 1852:

> *NEW STAGE LINE—Messrs. Hall & Crandall, the spirited proprietors of the San Jose mail line, have recently extended their sphere of usefulness even to the very center of the state, and we now find, through their exertions, San Francisco within 36 hours' drive of Shasta. The new line…between Sacramento and Shasta leave[s] daily…The line is well stocked with American horses, entire new trappings, and the finest Concord coaches. The proprietors of this enterprise have already given ample evidence, in the successful establishment of the San Jose and Monterey lines, of sufficient ability and experience to secure confidence and permanency in the one to which we allude. Messrs. Hall & Crandall have now upwards of three hundred miles of stage route in the State, over which their splendid coaches roll at least once a day.*

The firm's advertisements for the new line cited their "pledge to the traveling community that they [would] put them through with more expedition, more care, cheaper, and in better style than any line on this route" and assured the public that "the drivers employed on the line are all experienced in their business, and are temperate and responsible men, and passengers favoring this line may rely upon every attention being shown them." The company set up offices for the Shasta line at Sacramento's New Orleans Hotel; Berford & Company Express remained its agents.

The rough up-country roads were impassable by stage in the winter months, set-up costs were high and they faced established competition on the Colusa–Shasta line, but either the new ventures were sufficiently profitable or else the partners simply chose to concentrate on the "very center of the state," as the *Alta California* had applauded. In February 1853, Hall & Crandall sold its San Jose stage line to Dillon, Hedge & Company—experienced men who had also driven mail routes in New England and Mexico—and later in the year sold its San Francisco omnibus service to Crim & Sturgeon. Berford & Company stayed on as agents for Dillon-Hedge; Hall & Crandall appointed John S. Graham of Sacramento as its new agent.

Despite all due care and planning, not all of a stage operator's misfortunes arose from ordinary road hazards. In June 1853, Shasta City suffered a disastrous fire that consumed seventy buildings, destroying every hotel, mercantile, tradesmen's shop and saloon, sparing only about forty dwellings. The *Shasta Courier*—while acknowledging that many felt its estimate was too low—claimed the total loss at $500,000. Named among the heaviest losses was the $2,500 facility belonging to Hall & Crandall.

This loss notwithstanding, a month later Hall & Crandall announced additional summer arrangements for its daily mail stages leaving Sacramento's Crescent City Hotel, Orleans Hotel and Jackson Hall to connect with other coaches headed for Bidwell's Bar and the North Feather River mines; Park's Bar and Foster's Bar on the Yuba River north of Marysville; Nelson Creek and Sears' Diggings on the Yuba's north fork; and French Corral, nine miles northwest of Nevada City. Managing and supervising the business meant extensive travel and extended stays in the route's major cities; there are indications that Crandall was in Marysville for some time during the summer and fall of 1853 while his family home was still in Santa Clara County.

On September 5, 1853, the *Marysville Daily Herald* gushed over the firm's newest acquisition:

> *A MAGNIFICENT COACH.—One of the most superb six horse coaches that we ever remember to have seen, stopped in front of our office… for exhibition. It is of Concord (N.H.) manufacture, and was shipped to California as the property of Messrs. Hall & Crandall…who design placing it on the route between* [Sacramento and Marysville], *connecting with the Shasta regular line. This beautiful specimen of workmanship—as well for its excellent finish as great capacity—is capable of carrying 26 passengers…*[with luxurious accommodations for twelve inside and twelve comfortable seats outside]…*rendering the vehicle a species of juggernaut.*

The *Sacramento Union* chimed in on September 30 with a laudatory editorial:

> *STAGE ENTERPRISE.—The following complimentary notice of one of our most enterprising and energetic companies who afford land transit to interior travelers, is fully deserved, and receives our cordial endorsement. We quote from the* Catholic Standard*: This week an important addition has been made to the comfort and convenience of travelers…on Monday last four really magnificent coaches, carrying twenty-six passengers each, and drawn by six splendid horses, very richly harnessed, started from the Crescent City Hotel, Sacramento, for Marysville, Tehama and Shasta. Messrs. Hall & Crandall, the spirited proprietors of this line, deserve success, and we trust they will obtain it…On all their lines the agents are courteous gentlemen, and by their civility the passengers have given every satisfaction.*

Stagecoaches ascending the steep grade near Slippery Ford, circa 1860s. *Library of Congress, Lawrence & Houseworth Collection.*

Eight months later, J.B. Crandall and the Hall brothers announced the amicable dissolution of their co-partnership in a legal notice dated May 10, 1854, at San Jose following the absorption of Hall & Crandall's lines into James Birch's California Stage Company and Warren F. Hall's appointment as a trustee of that organization. Perhaps it was then, or shortly thereafter, that Jared Crandall relocated himself and his family to Placerville. There, in 1857, he was a co-owner of Crandall & Sunderland's Pioneer Stage Line operating between Folsom and Placerville.

By this time, the utter chaos of the early gold rush years had stabilized, although great numbers of immigrants were still arriving in wagons across Utah Territory, which then extended to California's eastern border. Mormon Station (later Genoa) was a busy trading post in the Carson River Valley. Inside California, communities from the already-flourishing to the up-and-coming wanted to enhance their resources and trading opportunities by attracting these new immigrants. The obvious answer to all was a widened and safer wagon road across the Sierra Nevada—moreover, one that led more or less directly into their own region. In April 1855, the state legislature had passed a bill to appropriate "not more than $5,000" to build a good road but without designating any specific route. Soon realizing that improvement costs would be far higher, the state surveyor general sent notices to "the friends of the various routes," and in early 1857, a spate of committees and wagon road conventions sprang up all over the northern districts to promote their individual choices and raise funds. Press coverage continued for weeks.

In the midst of all this controversy and wrangling, Jared Crandall took matters into his own hands. He stocked the worn trail east of Placerville with fresh teams, and on June 11, 1857, he departed Placerville at 3:15 a.m. for a dashing ride over Johnson's Pass with six Sacramento and Carson Valley Wagon Road directors (and one newspaper reporter) inside a nine-passenger Pioneer Stage Company mud wagon drawn by four horses. After breakfast at Sportsman's Hall—the farthest east a stagecoach had gone—Crandall's vehicle climbed upward to Strawberry Valley (now known as Kyburz), where all camped for the night. In the morning, Crandall crossed the dreaded, "insurmountable" Slippery Ford, sped around the south end of Lake Tahoe and arrived in Carson Valley that evening.

The newsman's very detailed report was euphoric: no accidents, and total travel time was less than twenty-eight hours! Ten days afterward, Jared Crandall established the first regular weekly mail and passenger stage service between Placerville and Genoa, upgraded to twice weekly after the more difficult portions of the road had been remedied. In September, Sacramento and El Dorado Counties voted to appropriate $25,000 each for further improvements. For all its later significance—with some modern-day variations, Crandall's celebrated jaunt is the route of today's Highway 50—he wasn't the first to cross the Sierra in a stagecoach. A week earlier, another contingent of wagon road delegates had gone out in a California Stage Company coach on a combined pleasure excursion/experimental expedition from Oroville to Honey Lake, although nothing came of it.

No one could possibly predict the discovery of titanic amounts of silver in Nevada. In the spring of 1858, shortly before news of this find became public, Crandall—now the sole owner—sold the Pioneer Stage Company to Lewis, Brady & Company, who established a semiweekly stage between Sacramento and Genoa. In August 1860, Crandall's buyers, by then reorganized as Brady & Sunderland, sold out to Louis McLane, the executive in charge of Wells Fargo & Company's operation in California.

Slippery Ford House, a hotel and stage stop. *Library of Congress, Lawrence & Houseworth Collection.*

Heavily used from the start, the Placerville–Carson Valley Road became even more densely packed as a heavy tide of population, freight wagons and stagecoaches poured eastward night and day into the Washoe region. From its early days, inns and stage stations only a few miles apart sprang up along the route to accommodate travelers: among them Pacific House, Fountain House, Strawberry Station and Yank's Station at Meyers Grade near Lake Tahoe. The most famed of these is still standing (albeit as a later reconstruction): Sportsman's Hall twelve miles east of Placerville, where seven daily stages stopped to change their teams. More than five hundred horses could be held in the stables and corrals west of the station, an impressive two-and-a-half-story building. The Pioneer Line was the dominant stagecoach service on this route through the next decade.

In June 1860, Jared Crandall and his family were still residing in Placerville, where he owned the Crandall & Company stage agency and

The first Sportsman's Hall, constructed in the early 1850s. The station burned twice and was immediately rebuilt each time. *Library of Congress, Lawrence & Houseworth Collection.*

evidently drove now and then for various stage lines. In November 1861, he was injured when the stage he was driving overturned, an accident attributed to his team of half-wild mustangs becoming frightened. Recovered by December, he drove T. Bradley's Accommodation Line stage from Placerville to Sacramento in "Good Time," as the *Union* cheered, beating the railroad passengers traveling the same route and assuring a reporter that the stage roads were still quite passable in mid-winter weather. Six years later, his son William was appointed as superintendent of Wells Fargo & Company's stagelines between Virginia City and California, in a few short months progressing to superintendent of both their Donner Lake and Placerville routes. Just when Jared Crandall returned to Santa Clara is unknown; however, the whole family was together there in June 1870, when the census taker knocked on their doors.

Jared Crandall was no longer young now and was surely suffering the physical effects common to all stage drivers after many hard years on the road in all types of weather. But he wouldn't—or couldn't—give up the reins altogether. Crandall was driving a Coast Line Stage Company coach when an accident took his life. Eight miles from Los Angeles, a wheel sank into a sand hole, throwing him from the box. Kicked by a frightened horse as he tumbled down, his skull was fractured as he struck the pole. Crandall took care of the team and, with the help of his lone passenger, attempted to right the toppled stage. Claiming to be unhurt he went to a nearby house to rest, where he died three hours later on November 24, 1872. The "prince of drivers" left a widow, three sons, a daughter-in-law, a toddler-aged grandson and a host of admirers.

LOUIS MCLANE: WELLS FARGO & COMPANY

Thirty-one-year-old ex–naval lieutenant Louis McLane Jr. landed in San Francisco in the spring of 1850 confident of the opportunities that awaited him in gold-fevered California, if somewhat anxious about leaving Sophie, his bride of ten months, back home in Maryland.

McLane had explored the Pacific coastline in 1844 as an acting lieutenant aboard the American naval vessel *Levant* when California was still a Mexican province. In 1847, he served in the Mexican-American War as commander of artillery of the California Battalion under the command of Lieutenant Colonel John Charles Fremont, U.S Army, and was appointed by Fremont as one of seven signatories to the Treaty of Cahuenga that ended the campaign on California soil. On both occasions, Louis was impressed with California's potential.

Energetic and self-disciplined, he was the descendant of a prominent Philadelphia-Baltimore clan and the son of former secretary of state Louis McLane. He had family money, connections and enough charisma to convince others to invest in his endeavors. With the financial backing of his father-in-law, Samuel Hoffman, Louis founded the California Steam Navigation Company, a firm that became a giant in waterways transportation. He returned home in 1852 for a yearlong stay, arriving by ship in New York five months before Wells Fargo & Company opened an express service in California.

The expressing business—defined as the rapid and safe movement of valuables by the fastest means available—was founded by William H. Hamden in 1839. In the early 1840s, Henry Wells and William G. Fargo separately began their careers as expressmen in upstate New York, each emerging as an important figure in the business by the end of the decade. Rather than combat new rival John Butterfield, they joined with him in 1850 to form the American Express Company. California beckoned as a potentially profitable new market, but Butterfield refused to extend services three thousand miles distant. William Fargo and Henry Wells gathered a group of investors and formed Wells, Fargo & Company in March 1852 to offer expressing, banking, gold buying and other related services on the West Coast. Other individuals took charge of operations, enabling Fargo and Wells to focus on their duties as officers and directors of American Express.

The new firm was a latecomer when it opened express offices in San Francisco and Sacramento simultaneously on July 13, 1852. Dozens of expresses had been operating since the latter half of 1849, but the common rival to all was Adams Express Company, which dominated the market. Hardly any of these expresses operated their own stage lines. They did not wish to invest in costly equipment or involve themselves in the daily complications of stocking relay stations or accommodating passengers.

Ignoring the modern pavement, this section of the stage road that was bypassed during construction of Highway 50 recollects the heyday of stagecoaching. *Photo by author.*

Instead, despite high transit rates, they preferred to contract with existing staging concerns to carry their strongboxes. Wells Fargo followed suit—providing another boon to stage operators.

The company established other branch offices in key California towns and bought out some of the smaller expresses, over the next three years advancing into second place behind Adams Express. In February 1855, the mighty Adams & Company's western venture suddenly collapsed, caught up short in the banking panic precipitated by the failure of its associate Page Bacon and Company, which shared the same building in San Francisco. Mobs of angry depositors stormed San Francisco's financial district, set on withdrawing their money from *any* bank before it, too, went under. The performance of Wells Fargo & Company during this crisis solidified its reputation for integrity and vaulted it into first place with a near monopoly on the express and banking business in the far West. This triumph notwithstanding, New York officials decided it was time to place a strong hand at the helm on the Pacific Coast. The company expected its agents to be knowledgeable and competent, to comport themselves like gentlemen and to meet the right people with whom they might participate in local civic affairs.

Louis McLane Jr. met all these standards and more. Besides the California Steam Navigation Company, McLane was a successful real estate developer in what later became Tehama County, a warehouse owner in bustling San Francisco and a director on the boards of a railroad enterprise and the Sacramento Gas Company. He was invested in mining interests, involved with the affairs of the Episcopal Church and was a generous contributor to various charities. On December 2, 1855, the *Daily Alta California* published the following announcement: "WELLS, FARGO & CO. To the Public. Louis McLane, Jr. is from this date General Agent for our House in California. Wells, Fargo & Company by T.M. Janes, Treasurer & Attorney."

From the start, expressing and stagecoaching in California had formed intimate bonds, one business complementing the interests of the other. As a premier express service, Wells Fargo awarded contracts to only the most reliable and well-equipped lines. Proud to be selected as a carrier, these stage operators in turn prominently lettered "Wells Fargo & Company's Express" on their coaches. In the public mind, every coach so lettered was a Wells Fargo coach, whether it really belonged to the Pioneer Stage Company or the California Stage Company or anyone else. This misconception was reinforced by newspapers, whose editors gratefully acknowledged receipt of other presses' publications (so they could copy and print their news items) as being "delivered by Wells Fargo Express," seldom if ever naming the actual stage line.

The Pioneer Line stage leaving Virginia City for Placerville. *Library of Congress, Lawrence & Houseworth Collection.*

By 1859, every stage that traveled to the rich silver veins in Nevada Territory was packed with prospectors. As a private business venture, Louis McLane purchased the profitable Pioneer Stage Company, announced in the August 29, 1860 issue of the *Sacramento Daily Union*:

> *NOTICE. THE ENTIRE PROPERTY AND GOOD WILL OF THE Pioneer Stage Company, on the route from Sacramento to Carson City, via Folsom and Placerville, heretofore belonging to Lewis Brady and Thomas Sunderland has this day been sold to Louis McLane. THOS. SUNDERLAND.*

Other Wells Fargo agents along the route handled Pioneer Stage business as part of their routine duties. As silver bars flowed westward from the Comstock and circulating gold coin flowed eastward, Wells Fargo's contracted transport fees to the stage company increased. Conflict of interest was not a concept in the nineteenth century, and Wells Fargo also benefited from McLane's investment, as seen in this advertisement in the June 4, 1864 *Sacramento Daily Union*:

> *PIONEER STAGE COMPANY. From Sacramento to Virginia City, Reese River, Humboldt and Salt Lake, carrying Wells, Fargo & Company's Express and the great Overland Mail to Atchison, Kansas, via Sacramento Valley Railroad to Folsom and thence by Stage to Placerville, Strawberry Valley, Lake Valley, Genoa, Carson City, Silver City, Dayton, Washoe City. Gold Hill and Virginia* [City]—*connecting at Genoa for Markleeville, Monitor, Silver Mountain and Aurora. Passengers by this Line have a beautiful view of Lake Bigler* [Lake Tahoe]—*and by the FIRST OF JULY will connect with Cars at Latrobe (Miller's Corral), on the Placerville and Sacramento Valley Railroad, eighteen miles above Folsom—shortening the distance and time of arrival in Placerville three hours; and on completion of the South Fork Road up the American river* [sic] *from Blakeley's to Webster's, will be able to land passengers in Virginia City by ten P.M. same day of leaving Sacramento. Office of the Company: WHAT CHEER HOUSE, corner Front and K Streets. LOUIS McLANE & COMPANY, Proprietors.*

Meanwhile, John Butterfield, who had snatched the southern-routed overland mail contract from James Birch in 1857, found himself in financial difficulties and worse. As the secession crisis heated up, Congress mandated a central mail route in March 1861 to run through Salt Lake City. In a maze of transactions stemming from private and government interests, Utah staging impresario Ben Holladay acquired the central overland mail contract from Utah east to the Missouri River, with Wells Fargo & Company to carry the mail from Salt Lake City west. One segment of the route covered the distance from Folsom to booming Virginia City, Nevada, a segment that was subcontracted to the Pioneer Stage Company. In December 1864, Wells Fargo & Company purchased the Pioneer Line from its employee Louis McLane, and eight months later, it bought the California Stage Company's route over Donner Pass. Wells Fargo & Company now outright owned stagelines at last but retained the Pioneer name for its excellent reputation.

In another private venture in October 1865, McLane formed a consortium to purchase the California Stage Company's 700-mile line from Sacramento to Portland, Oregon, but less than a year later, Portland businessman Henry

A Wells Fargo & Company Concord coach used for its Overland Mail Service in the 1860s. *Author's collection.*

Corbett acquired both the mail contract and the California-Oregon Stage Company. At the pinnacle of his staging endeavors, Louis McLane was invested in 6,800 miles of stagecoaching, through his privately owned lines and financial interests in others.

Sometime during the months of September and October 1866, Wells Fargo & Company successfully ousted Ben Holladay—at great cost in cash and stock—and gained full control of all the express business conducted by the Overland Mail Company between the Missouri River and the Pacific Ocean. Louis McLane ascended to the presidency of Wells Fargo & Company on November 1, 1866. The *Daily Alta* exclaimed, "Louis McLane...one of the most active organizers of California prosperity...a large owner in Wells, Fargo...goes East to superintend the affairs of the Company in New York." McLane and his wife and six children booked passage on the eastbound steamer *Sacramento*.

Yet McLane—for all his considerable expertise—could not control outside influences. In the mid-1860s, cheaper freight and passenger costs offered by the advancing Central Pacific Railroad began to erode staging revenues from the fabulous Comstock while expenses on the overland mail route grew to enormous proportions, and Wells Fargo's stock plummeted 60 percent. Outlining the company's poor financial condition at the May 1868 board of directors meeting, McLane then tendered his resignation with the explanation that his private interests in California required his personal attention. Wells Fargo's burnished cherry-red Concord coaches rumbled across the central prairies until they were usurped by the completion of the first transcontinental railroad in 1869, although the company's express and banking services inside California and Oregon continued for decades thereafter. Louis McLane went on to develop and head other prestigious firms in California and Nevada. He died in 1905, at age eighty-six, at his large estate in Baltimore, Maryland.

PART III

HAZARDS OF THE ROAD

A Test of Endurance

A ride in a California stagecoach was nothing at all like a sedate pleasure outing in a private buggy. "Don't imagine for a moment you are going on a picnic," warned one newspaper. "Expect annoyance, discomfort, and some hardships."

A "through" passenger traveled to the end of the line, and a "way" passenger disembarked at stations along the route. Regardless of distance, most fretted over a long list of potential hazards, from overflowed creeks to overturned vehicles, whether from past experience or the reports of others. Stage horses trotting through alpine regions sometimes attracted the interest of bears and mountain lions. Lost luggage was not uncommon, as evidenced by the "Lost and Found" columns of period newspapers.

Once on board, the coach was confining, a situation made more awkward when hoop skirts were fashionable from the late 1850s to the mid-1860s, as seating room inside a Concord was only about fifteen inches per person. A nine-passenger Concord contained three leather-cushioned seats. Those at the front and back of the coach faced each other, and the one in the center faced forward. Only the end seats had padded back cushions; the backrest for the center bench was a broad leather belt suspended on straps from the ceiling. Long-legged travelers who faced each other had to interlock knees, and sometimes mail bags were thrust between passengers' feet. Unruly children frequently annoyed male passengers, and the ladies complained of the gentlemen's cigar smoke wafting through the interior. Both genders

Team and passengers enjoy a temporary halt to pose for the camera, circa 1890s. *Author's collection.*

related their discomfort at being forcibly squeezed between corpulent or foul-breathed fellow travelers. Many chose to ride on the roof instead, an option not available in cloth-topped mud wagons.

A stagecoach could travel up to twelve miles an hour over flat, hard surfaces, slowing to two miles per hour or less going up inclines or over steep downgrades. On these occasions, the driver might ask passengers to get out and push (ladies excepted) or stand by the roadside while the coach half slid down to more level ground. "As the road became less level, it became us as human beings to relieve the poor beasts by an occasional walk up steep hills," one lady reported. "I dragged my weary feet, for the moment puffing like a steamer." At a mere five or six miles per hour, a stagecoach thoroughly exhausted its passengers, who clung to anything that promised stability as they bounced about, doubtless in complete agreement with author Bret Harte's acerbic opinion. Writing some twenty years after the advent of staging in the Golden State, Harte recalled a time when "lunatics had not reached such depths of imbecility as to ride of their own free will in California stages."

HAZARDS OF THE ROAD

The only stage that didn't punish head and limb was the sleigh, limited to winter travel through the higher elevations. These first came into use in late 1860. Said the *Marysville Herald*:

> *The old bugbear of snow in the Sierra Nevada which used to be thought an insuperable objection to all schemes for regular winter travel between the Eastern and Western slopes, and the regions lying north of California, has at last been pretty much dissipated by the energy of a few businessmen. It is proposed to keep the Henness Pass route to Washoe open...running sleds between near stations at frequent intervals. Arrangements have already been made for sled travel on the Placerville route.*

Sleighs glided rapidly and smoothly over packed snow with seldom an unpleasant jar, drawn by horses shod with special shoes of metal squares with rubber attached to the bottom. Passengers were so delighted with this mode of staging that they were disappointed when changing terrain meant a transfer back to a "regular" coach.

Still, many travelers—mostly young men—found adventure and exhilaration in a clattering, rocking stagecoach and were quite willing to ignore inconveniences.

Concords manufactured for California roads had no glazed windows, lest the glass shatter. Mud wagons had canvas sides that were usually rolled up. The Concord's leather curtains and the mud wagon's fastened-down cloth panels shielded passengers from inclement weather but effectively left them in the dark. Neither curtains nor panels kept freezing cold from seeping in; winter travelers bundled themselves in heavy coats, gloves, wool scarves and lap blankets, adding extra bulk to already crowded conditions. Summer weather brought other discomforts. Travelers aboard open-paneled mud wagons suffered less stifling conditions, but the interior of a Concord heated to the level of a low-degree oven. Then there was the dust, constantly kicked up by the horses' hooves. It filled the air, permeating luggage, hats, hair and skin, at times covering passengers so thoroughly that everyone's clothing and faces were one grimy color.

Further, stagecoach tickets were expensive, and meals at home stations cost extra. Quite often this was poor fare, devoid of dairy products or fruit.

Roads were little more than trails when staging began in California during the chaotic gold rush. Clearing brush and grading required a substantial workforce, and gold miners in the early days were loath to waste their time earning wages when they might find their hoped-for

North American Hotel on the western summit, Placerville route. *Library of Congress, Lawrence & Houseworth Collection.*

bonanza today or tomorrow. By the end of the 1850s, however, many routes featured improved roads.

A traveler passing over one such widened and improved roadbed between Placerville and Gold Hill, Nevada, during the Comstock's heyday penned his experience for the *San Francisco Call-Bulletin.* He was a passenger on Louis McLane's Pioneer Stage Line:

> *The mountain roads (via the Pioneer route) were very solid, and better than many anticipated. Staging they called first-rate. Well, it might be so to those who like it, but it is heavy on the insides. This trip showed up the value of our bullion trade to travelers, and the difference between going up and coming down. Going down there is generally plenty of bullion in the stage, which keeps it steady and makes the ride easy. Going up, if there be a light load, the stage tumbles about on the rough roads like a ship in a storm, and it is just as necessary to have the passengers lashed down. I never got such a tumbling,*

Yank's Station, the easternmost stage stop in California on the Placerville Road, operated by Ephraim "Yank" Clements. It became Meyers in 1873. *Library of Congress, Lawrence & Houseworth Collection.*

bruising, bumping, and thumping in all my life. Orders were given to "make Strawberry at 3 P.M.," and they made it easy—for the stages, but horribly uneasy for the poor passengers. I would suggest to Louis McLane to have holes cut through the top of the stage, so that when your head does go up it can go through far enough to give you a chance to swear at the driver for taking such pains to hit every rock in the road. Sometimes, if you could see out, you would think they were driving through a fallen forest and over trees six feet thick.

This unknown correspondent suffered no great mishaps on his journey except for a number of unpleasant jolts when the stage wheels hit a chuckhole. Other passengers on other roads were not as fortunate. Reports of Indian attacks on coaches in the northern counties and highwaymen who might strike anywhere instilled apprehension in everyone who needed to travel by stagecoach.

Accidents

Considering the thousands of miles the stagecoach rumbled over northern California, accidents were actually rare—yet when they did happen, the results ranged from traumatized passengers to complete disaster. The worst incidents involved a capsized coach.

No one was hurt when an ascending stage struck a log near Goodyears Bar and broke every spoke in the wheels. The *Marysville Daily Herald* reported a severe injury to a Shasta resident when a team leader's sudden fright upset a Hall & Crandall stage on level ground. Two passengers suffered a delirium-producing concussion and a compound fracture of the leg when the inbound stage from Nevada City entered Sacramento at a too rapid pace and overturned at the corner of E and Eleventh Streets, but in the same year, no bones were broken when a large six-horse coach of the California Stage Company upset on a run between Sacramento and Marysville.

The brake bar on the Placerville stage broke off while descending a heavy grade in the vicinity of Diamond Springs, allowing the vehicle to crowd the horses—inciting them to bolt and run. Driver H.F. Page did his best, but a short distance farther on, the out-of-control animals rounded a short curve, throwing the vehicle on its side. Page and his one outside passenger were "considerably scratched," and the seven inside were shaken, but the only death was one of the horses, which had to be shot. Two coaches filled with passengers upset almost simultaneously near Sportsman's Hall above Placerville when the front stage hit a stump and capsized. The stage behind stopped to render assistance, but then its team shied, sending the second coach over a bank. Injuries were classified as critical. A Pioneer Line stage, going down a grade at full speed about twelve miles beyond Strawberry Station, met a fast freight wagon coming up. It was February, and the road was icy. The Pioneer stage's wheels slipped off an embankment and went over a precipice, coach and team rolling downhill forty or fifty feet. Remarkably, no one was killed or even seriously injured.

One of the most catastrophic mishaps occurred on October 19, 1861, on the mountain road winding out of Downieville.

At three o'clock in the morning, a California Stage Company coach was ascending the Goodyear Hill when, in making a very short turn on the narrowest portion of the road, the ground beneath the hind wheel gave way, causing the wheel to slip over the embankment.

Driver Miles Nesmith immediately whipped up his team. For a few moments, the stage was poised on the brink of the precipice—then the rapidly

Strawberry Stage Station on the Placerville route, 1860s. *Library of Congress Lawrence & Houseworth Collection.*

crumbling ground pitched vehicle, horses, driver and passengers into the abyss below. The coach shattered into countless fragments; three of the horses were dead when they reached the bottom. Miles Nesmith fell more than one hundred yards and was badly injured. Of the six passengers inside, two were killed outright, one died shortly afterward and the others were "more or less mangled," as the news story stated. One of the two passengers sitting outside beside the driver became lodged in some bushes about fifty yards down, unhurt except for multiple cuts and scratches. The other attempted to jump from the stage, became entangled in the reins, fell among the horses and rolled with them about three hundred yards. He was not expected to live but did. The Green & Company stage, coming along several minutes after the accident, transported the wounded to the Mountain House, a sizable inn and stage stop a mile away on the Henness Pass Road at the junction of the road leading north to Goodyears Bar and south to Forest City.

A coach and six horses hurtling down a mountain. *Library of Congress, from a 1904 painting by Frederic Remington.*

Six years later, the *Daily Alta California* reported the "Coffee Creek Disaster" in Trinity County in early December when a flash flood of five or six feet suddenly engulfed a stagecoach as it was trying to cross. The driver was swept some two hundred yards away, where he caught onto a stump, from there working his way to an island formed by the slough on one side and the creek on the other. After shedding his drenched outer clothing, he walked several miles for help, reaching a house after being exposed to the elements for nine hours in a storm. The *Alta* speculated that the sudden rise of water in the creek was caused when a large body of accumulated water high in the mountains was let loose by a slide of melting snow. At the date of the news story ten days after the incident, the body of a drowned passenger had been recovered, but the treasure box of Wells Fargo & Company containing $2,000 was still missing.

The following year, a Green & Company sleigh used for staging purposes, coming down the Goodyears Bar hill on runners, flipped and rolled several hundred feet into a ravine after the snow suddenly caved under it. Driver Warren Green, the only person in the sleigh at the time, was cut and bruised, but he and his horses escaped serious injury.

Some incidents were unusual.

Stagecoach transport was booming in 1850, when Ezra Sherwood, brother-in-law of future railroad baron Mark Hopkins, was returning home to Marysville from Sacramento after nightfall on the Fourth of July, seated on the roof of a coach. A tree limb projecting across the road struck him in the head, killing him instantly. Stagecoach travel was lessening in 1904, when a stage driver averted a potential calamity-in-the-making, as reported in the *Amador Ledger*, copying the *Redding Free Press*:

> A great big rattlesnake with body coiled, rattles buzzing, head erect and fangs sticking out in a threatening way held up the southbound Redding and Weaverville stage on Niagara Hill Wednesday and Stage Driver Dick Heath was compelled to climb down from his seat and kill the rattler before the stage [horses] could go by.

THE PITT RIVER INDIAN ATTACK

In late August 1856, stage driver Jared "Curly Jerry" Robbins left the Pitt River station on his way south to Red Bluff. He had no passengers. A great

Stage driving brothers "Curly Dan" and "Curly Jerry" Robbins. *Author's collection.*

portion of the route was through timber and chaparral and then passed over a stretch of thirty miles of waterless wilderness. Several miles down this lonely and desolate route, a shower of arrows suddenly rained in upon Robbins from the thick bushes that lined each side of the road. With many arrows sticking in his clothes and flesh, Curly Jerry cracked his whip, commanding his team to run. The horses, also hit by arrows, were so frightened that they sped over the ground in a headlong flight that threatened to capsize the coach or smash it to pieces against stumps and rocks. The arrows kept coming.

At length—Robbins was never sure of the time or distance—he reached a small open prairie where there was no cover for the ambushers, but here the battered coach suddenly broke down. Leaping from his seat, Jerry unhitched the terrified animals just as loud yells signaled a charge from the attackers. He sprang on the back of one of the horses, grabbed the reins of the others and once again dashed away at high speed. Passing the prairie, the team again plunged into the dangerous chaparral where the ambush continued, riddling Jerry's clothes and gloves with arrows. Although covered with blood, Jerry urged his animals on, encouraged by the thought that he was getting closer to the Hat Creek Station some ninety miles northeast of Red Bluff. The shooting gradually slackened as he neared this post. Curly Jerry arrived at the door wounded in sixteen places but survived with the aid of a Shasta City doctor.

Just a month earlier, the California Stage Company had opened this road from Red Bluff to Yreka, taking passengers through from Sacramento to Yreka in three days. A month after this incident, the company closed the route.

ROAD RAGE

Premier stage companies usually inserted assurances in their advertisements that their drivers were safe, reliable and courteous. The California Stage Company, widely acknowledged for its excellent service, employed the wrong man when it hired Oscar Case.

Not every northern California stage line was swept up in James Birch's grand consolidation, and over time new ones appeared, publicly declaring themselves as "the opposition." As such, Fowler & Company ran a small line from Marysville to Sacramento. A week before the "Unfortunate Affair"—as the *Sacramento Daily Union* headlined the life-threatening confrontation—Fowler & Company hired J. Stinchfield as a driver.

On the morning of November 14, 1858, Stinchfield started out with his stage as usual. About six miles south of Marysville, Oscar Case came racing up behind him, driving a heavy Troy-manufactured coach drawn by older and steadier horses than Stinchfield's team. As soon as Case was near enough, he began throwing firecrackers at the Fowler stage, scaring its horses into a near unmanageable state. Next, Case ran his stage into Stinchfield's lighter-weight mud wagon, breaking some of its spokes and knocking down one of its horses. After this, both stages continued to the Twelve Mile House below Marysville. Stinchfield's passenger L.H. Ruby later testified:

I was outside on the box; Oscar Case was on the coach of the California Stage Company right opposite. As soon as we started out he went right ahead of us, stopped his team, and whenever our driver attempted to pass by he would haul in front of us; he continued to do so until we got to the Twelve Mile House. [All of us] *stopped there...he overtook us just this side of the Bear River bridge...and run us out of the road.* [We] *went out off the road, across a field; we saw no more of Case until we got about two miles below Nicolaus...Case then came running up with a fresh team of horses and tried to run us into a fence, and hauled in front of us again; whenever we attempted to go by he would run us off the road, sometimes half a mile. He continued to do so until we got to Grey's Rancho. When we got there I had a talk with him and tried to dissuade him from acting in the way he did. He said he intended to run into the coach before we could get to Sacramento...He said he was paid to do it, to run off the Opposition, break up the coaches,* [and] *raise the devil generally. He said they had given him that old coach and good horses to wipe out the Opposition in any way that he could...*

Further witnesses testified that Stinchfield and his several passengers all repeatedly asked Case to leave them alone, yet he persisted.

After the first assault, a Fowler passenger named Ames had borrowed a double-barreled shotgun at an earlier stop and was quite serious about using it should Oscar Case continue his attempts to overturn the Fowler stage. From then on, he, too, rode outside next to the driver. During the brief stopover at the Twelve Mile House, Case—either having worked himself into a fury or just crazy—verbally threatened the Fowler stage passengers with death before they reached Sacramento unless they left the Fowler coach and boarded his own. Both coaches were below Nicolaus, with Case's hind wheel locked to Stinchfield's front wheel, when Ames—after yelling at Case to get out of the way several times—fired the shotgun.

Case turned his horses in pursuit of Ames, who had bolted into the surrounding tules immediately after shooting. But as the Fowler stage escaped toward Sacramento to protect its safety and report the incident, Oscar Case headed back toward Marysville. Too wounded to continue, he got down from his seat and collapsed near the road, where he was found a short time afterward by two men on horseback. They took him to a private residence in Nicolaus, where he gave a concerned visitor an edited version of the story. He said that a Fowler stage passenger had threatened to shoot him several times after leaving Marysville; that the two stages had locked

A coach-and-six on a lonely road. *Courtesy California State Library, Sacramento.*

wheels; and that he supposed Ames only intended to strike him with the gun since he (Case) was alone, unarmed and had four horses to take care of while there was a sufficient number of male passengers in the Fowler stage to "do with him whatever they wanted" without shooting him.

Ames was acquitted November 26 in what the judge declared was a clear case of self-defense. Oscar Case died on December 23. A coroner's inquest recorded the facts of the homicide, but no inquiry was made into the motives or state of mind of the deceased—or who, if anyone, might have paid him to "wipe out" another's business. The Sacramento and San Francisco press opined that the entire affray was rooted in strong provocation growing from the rivalry between the "old" and the "new" stage lines. The California Stage Company made no public statement.

PART IV

STAGE ROBBERIES

In the early years of the California gold rush, stagecoaches transported more than $100 million in gold from widely spread hinterland camps to big-city safes, through lonely forests and over winding back roads without incident. Robberies did occur, of course. In the Marysville Wells Fargo office, a man set his bag containing $400 on the counter while he wrote at the desk. When he looked back, the satchel was gone. A stage driver headed for Stockton was three miles out of Sonora, checking his baggage load before crossing the river, when he discovered that the Adams & Company express box containing $25,000 in gold had been stolen from the back boot of the coach before the vehicle left Sonora. The express bag of Rhodes & Lusk was stolen from the sidewalk in front of Wells Fargo & Company's office in Sacramento minutes after it had been thrown down from the Shasta stage. These three thefts took place between 1853 and 1855; several more were reported in the mining camps and in the business offices of stage companies and express agents.

But it was not until 1856 that anyone had the sheer audacity to hold up a moving stagecoach.

HIGHWAYMAN TOM BELL

On August 12, the Camptonville stage was nearing the fork in the road that would take it into Marysville. The coach was carrying the Langton &

Reenactment of a stage robbery, circa 1911. *Library of Congress, Prints &*
Photograph Division.

Company's treasure box containing $100,000 in gold and several passengers, including Bill Dobson, Langton's armed express messenger. At about four thirty in the afternoon, six masked, mounted men suddenly appeared from behind a thicket and ordered driver John Gear to stop the stage, threatening to kill the first man who opposed them. Dobson, who was seated outside next to Gear, immediately drew on the highwaymen and commenced firing, striking and unhorsing their spokesman. A volley of forty or more rapid shots followed, fired by both sides, and in the confusion, the robbers sped away. John Gear was shot through his right arm above the elbow. One passenger received a glancing shot over his eye, and another was shot in both legs. Mrs. Tilghman, wife of a Marysville barber, died instantly from a shot through the head. Though badly injured, John Gear snapped the reins, and the stage sped on to Marysville with the treasure box intact.

The prime suspect in the Camptonville stage holdup was Tom Bell, the rumored leader of a gang of toughs who had ranged the gold region for months, terrorizing miners and peddlers, robbing stores and stealing livestock. Only the previous June, a man named Samuel Rosenthal had disappeared while traveling between Grass Valley and Folsom. He was thought to be carrying a large amount of cash and was presumed murdered. The robbery of a soda wagon driver was reported, too. Both incidents occurred in the vicinity of a tavern between Auburn and Folsom called the Mountaineer House, and both were attributed to Tom Bell.

Bell's real name was Thomas J. Hodges. Born about 1826, he came from a respectable Tennessee family and was well educated. He served as a medical orderly during the Mexican-American War with the Tennessee Volunteers and then, in 1850, migrated to California, where his life soon went awry. A year later, he was caught after a horse-stealing raid and sentenced to state prison, which at that time was the converted ship *Waban* anchored at Angel Island in San Francisco Bay. There, Hodges met three other inmates who would form the nucleus of his robber gang: Jim Smith, Bill Gristy (alias Bill White) and Edward (Ned) Connor. The four escaped and commenced preying on isolated mining camps and mountain travelers. Hodges may have adopted the alias Tom Bell at this time simply to confound the law because there was another horse thief by that name roaming the area.

The confusion didn't last long, however. Lawmen knew about the state prison escapes and had already identified Bill Gristy as one of a band that had burglarized the Rhodes & Whitney Express offices in Marysville the previous April. Further, they had Tom Bell's description: he was tall and wiry, with a full head of sandy-colored hair and a matching mustache and goatee. His eyes were light blue, and his nose was smashed at the bridge almost level with his face. "Sightings" from all over Nevada, Yuba and Placer Counties appeared in the press as soon as his description was circulated, along with excited reports that the renegade was brazenly flaunting his identity while boasting he would never be caught. Acting on tips and hunches, sheriffs from different jurisdictions joined forces. By September 18, most of the Bell gang had been killed in desperate shootouts or arrested. Tom Bell was still at large.

Arrested near Knight's Ferry in Stanislaus County, Bill Gristy was only too happy to confess the details of the Camptonville stage holdup and other crimes, as well as promise to lead officers to Bell's hideout—a deserted ranch near the Tulare Slough 120 miles below Stockton. Two groups converged on the location, and after a frustrating weeklong wait, they were in the process of dispersing when one man, purely by accident, spotted a rider hidden in a clump of willows. He alerted the others, who went back to investigate,

Knight's Ferry in the early nineteenth century. *Library of Congress, Lawrence & Houseworth Collection.*

and they captured Tom Bell an hour before noon on October 4, 1856. A rider was sent after Sheriff Mulford, who had departed the scene sometime earlier with the official posse. However, upon further discussion, the captors realized that if they waited for Mulford's return, the sheriff would most likely insist on taking the prisoner to jail, an outcome none of them wanted. They hanged Tom Bell at five o'clock.

Irresistible Temptation

Despite the widely publicized execution of Bell, the stiff prison terms his accomplices received and the undeniable fact that—after all—the Camptonville stage robbery had failed, the very idea that a traveling stagecoach *might* be forced to surrender its treasure chest seemed to inspire a long list of the more ambitious criminally inclined. A closed door had been flung open.

STAGE ROBBERIES

Six months after the Camptonville episode, in February 1857, three highwaymen held up the Stockton stage carrying an accumulation of express from three mining camps and made off with $30,000 in gold dust. They were captured within a day and the treasure boxes of Wells Fargo and Pacific Express Company recovered. This was the second stage holdup. The number of stage robberies escalated in the 1860s, reached the highest levels in the 1870s and 1880s and persisted into the next century. Wells Fargo & Company adopted a proactive policy: it promptly reimbursed its customers for stolen express shipments, offered rewards and, in the late 1860s, assembled an in-house detective force. James B. Hume, who served from 1873 until his death in 1904, was its best-known special officer.

Temptation attracted all classes of thieves to the stage-robbing business, even those who were clearly inept. In April 1866, the *Sacramento Daily Union* quoted a dispatch from another city:

> *The stage for Marysville was stopped this afternoon...by three men who came out from behind trees. They were armed with double-barreled guns and revolvers, and had their faces blackened. Only one passenger on board. The robbers searched him, the driver and the stage, but overlooked the treasure box and did not get a cent.*

Two stagecoach robberies five days apart made headlines in 1864, while the Civil War still raged. No lives were lost on June 25, when the stage from Bidwell's Bar to Oroville was stopped by a party of highwaymen who ordered driver Charles Wykoff to hand over the Whiting & Company's express box. The robbers broke open the box, extracted $1,885 in coin and threw the box back into the stage before leaving with their take. Members of the notorious Gassaway family (known to be the robbers of the Langton's Express at an earlier date), together with two cohorts and the wife and daughter-in-law of Upton Gassaway, were arrested and the men jailed. The women were charged bail of $100 each as accessories to the crimes. On Thursday, June 30, two Pioneer Line stages carrying Wells Fargo & Company's express from Carson, Nevada, filled with fourteen passengers each, were simultaneously held up a few miles east of Placerville by radical Confederate sympathizers. The aftermath was one dead, a standing-room-only trial and a spot on the stage road still known as Bullion Bend.

RENEGADE CONFEDERATES

Drivers Ned Blair and Charley Watson had left Carson City in the morning but now it was ten o'clock at night, and the only light on the narrow mountain road came from the Concords' candle lamps as they clattered down the hill from Strawberry Station. Watson rounded a bend to suddenly find Blair's stage stopped ahead of him. Thinking some accident had occurred, Watson reined up, too—and was confronted by the same six armed men who had just stolen twelve silver bars and a small quantity of gold from Blair's coach. The gang ordered Blair to go on, but as Blair's vehicle was starting out, an off-duty police officer passenger fired two shots from inside. This so enraged the road agents that they threatened to shoot Watson and all of his passengers. Charley Watson coolly replied that since no shot had been fired from *his* stage, no harm ought to be done to his passengers.

At this point, one of the gang claiming to be the leader stepped forward with an explanation: "Gentlemen, I will tell you who we are. We are not robbers but a company of Confederate soldiers. Don't act foolish. We don't want anything of the passengers. All we want is Wells Fargo & Company's treasure, to assist us to recruit for the Confederate army."

Today, Bullion Bend's curve dead-ends beneath modern Highway 50. *Photo by author.*

Charley Watson threw out two sacks. One of the robbers got up on the boot and confiscated another sack of silver bullion and a small box of express freight. Watson was handed a pre-written, incomplete receipt that said, "June __ 1864, This is to certify that I have received from Wells Fargo & Company the sum of ___$ cash, ___for the purpose of outfitting recruits enlisted in California for the Confederate States army. HENRY M. INGRAHAM, Captain Commanding Company, C.S.A."

Considerable agitation ensued when both stages convened at Placerville, and a posse started out immediately. Two of the robbers were discovered in their beds before sunrise at the Thirteen Mile House, a traveler's way station east of Sportsman's Hall. Deputy Sheriff Joseph Staples and Constable George Ranney found three of the highwaymen holed up at Somerset House, a hostelry in southern Placer County on the cutoff that led to Grizzly Flat. Ranney wisely refrained from direct confrontation, but Deputy Staples burst into their room shouting, "You are my prisoners—surrender!" He was answered with a barrage of gunfire that killed him and wounded Constable Ranney.

Captain Ingraham (also known as Rufus Henry Ingraham) fled the state and was never found. A Santa Clara resident who had aided and abetted

Historical marker—"In Memory of the Bravery of Our Pioneer Officers"—at the site of the 1864 Bullion Bend stage robbery. *Photo by author.*

the gang but was not personally involved in the stage holdup was sentenced to twenty years as an accessory to the murder of Deputy Joseph Staples. Thomas B. Poole, a former undersheriff of Monterey County who had been an active participant in the robbery and one of the men who shot at Staples in the Somerset House, was hanged on September 29, 1865.

Robbing stages en route was not an avocation for the fainthearted; it required careful planning and steady nerves. Heavy coaches traveling at a smart clip created their own momentum, and high-strung stage horses were known to take fright and bolt at sudden surprises. Knowledgeable road agents waited behind cover until the vehicle naturally slowed to ascend or descend a grade before leaping out to grab the leaders' reins or simply command the driver to halt. Between July 1875 and November 1883, a lone holdup man fearlessly—and with obvious skill and forethought—robbed twenty-eight coaches, all carrying Wells Fargo strongboxes. His astonishing scope of operations ranged hundreds of miles from Calaveras County into southern Oregon. In between, he hit up stages in Yuba, Siskiyou, Sonoma, Butte, Shasta, Mendocino, Plumas, Nevada and Amador Counties. He later said his alias was inspired by a dime novel titled *The Case of Summerfield*, whose author resurrected Captain Henry Ingraham of Bullion Bend stage robbery fame as a fictional, unruly villain named Black Bart.

HIGHWAYMAN CHARLES BOWLES, AKA BLACK BART

It was a lovely summer morning on July 26, 1875, when driver John Shine set out from Sonora on his regular stage run to Copperopolis and Milton. He carried five passengers inside and the Wells Fargo Express strongbox at his feet, containing $300 in gold dust. After crossing the Stanislaus River on Reynold's ferry, Shine's team made the long, slow climb up Funk's Hill. Suddenly, a figure clad from shoulders to heels in a linen duster slipped from behind a roadside boulder, crouched in front of the startled leaders and aimed a double-barreled shotgun at Shine's head. A flour sack slit with peepholes masked his face. The assailant's deep voice tersely commanded Shine to throw down the treasure box, which he did after quickly looking about and seeing what he thought were several shotguns sticking out from the bushes. As the box hit the ground, the robber stood up, looking to be over six feet tall. He came back toward the coach with quick, springy steps, demanding the mail sacks. Shine's female passenger panicked and tossed her satchel out the window. The robber bowed courteously and returned it to the lady, declaring that he only wanted the goods belonging to Wells Fargo. Gathering up his loot, the highwayman ordered Shine to "hurry along" and faded into the brush.

Lawmen rushed to the scene, where they discovered that the "shotguns" Shine had seen were merely sticks artfully stuck between the boulders, a trick that the clever bandit would repeat on his next holdup in Yuba County on December 28, 1875, one hundred miles north of Funk's Hill. On June 2, 1876, an identical stage robbery occurred in Siskiyou County, more than two hundred miles farther north. In each case, the description of the robber was the same: he was six feet tall, physically agile, had a deep voice and spoke perfect English. He wore a flour sack over his face, appeared to be on foot and left no other clues except for a taunting bit of poetic drivel scrawled on the back of a Wells Fargo waybill that he left at the scene of his fourth robbery near Duncans Mills (Sonoma County) in August 1877:

> *Here I lay me down to sleep*
> *To wait the coming morrow,*
> *Perhaps success, perhaps defeat*
> *And everlasting sorrow.*
> *I've labored long and hard for bread*
> *For honor and for riches*
> *But on my corns too long you've tread*
> *You fine haired Sons of Bitches.*
> *Yet come what will, I'll try it once,*
> *My conditions can't be worse,*
> *And if there's money in that box,*
> *'Tis money in my purse.*
> *Black Bart, the Po8*

Now the mysterious bandit had a name. Accumulating bits of meager information, Wells Fargo's chief of detectives Jim Hume deduced that the suspect was a tall, educated young man with extensive mountaineering experience. But after interviewing everyone in the vicinity of each incident, no tall, young stranger on foot had been seen. Indians hired by the Mendocino County sheriff after the first two robberies there in October 1878 lost his trail after sixty miles. These expert trackers reported that the

Artist's rendition of Black Bart. *Author's collection.*

fugitive was a tireless walker through extremely rugged country; could not be more than five feet, eight inches tall; and did no hunting or cooking but lived on crackers and sugar.

Hume sent his entire detective force into the area where the trail had been lost, but the only reported stranger was a traveling preacher who had stopped for a meal at the McCreary farmhouse. Mrs. McCreary emphatically denied that her visitor could have been the infamous Black Bart. Why, he was a kindly older gentleman only two inches taller than she, wearing shabby clothes and old shoes. His eyes were blue, and his hair, mustache and a little tuft of beard on his chin were snow white. Yes, he had a deep voice. He hadn't *said* he was a preacher—Mrs. McCreary had determined this based on his "intellectual conversation" while he ate. She did notice that his two front teeth were missing.

During the next two years, Black Bart executed seven stage holdups, in three instances a pair of them in quick succession in the same area. The investigation of yet another holdup near Redding in 1881 produced a farmer who said that a stranger answering Mrs. McCreary's exact description had stopped at his cabin for breakfast. Convinced now that the old gentleman was indeed the phantom robber, and after analyzing the pattern of holdups, Jim Hume further deduced that he lived in a big city—probably San Francisco—and robbed stages only when he was short of money. Hume's theory turned out to be accurate.

In 1881 and 1882, Black Bart held up eight more stages with impunity; the ninth try on July 13, 1882, nearly ended his career. Bart had scarcely stepped out in front of the team before Wells Fargo messenger George Hackett, who was guarding a $23,000 treasure, fired with a near-miss that partially ripped off Bart's flour sack mask as the highwayman fled through the bushes, and the spooked horses galloped away with the stage before Hackett could jump down from the box. Undaunted, Bart robbed the Redding-Yreka stage two months later, struck twice near Cloverdale in the spring of 1883 and held up the Ione stage near Jackson that June.

Black Bart's last robbery took place at the scene of his first, at Funk's Hill in Calaveras County. An hour before dawn on November 3, 1883, stage driver Reason McConnell left Tuttletown headed for Copperopolis with a Wells Fargo strongbox containing $4,815 bolted to the floor inside the coach. Stopping for breakfast at a little inn, McConnell agreed to take the innkeeper's nineteen-year-old son, Jimmy, along to Copperopolis so the young man could hunt deer behind the ridge at Funk's Hill. The team slowed to a walk at the foot of the hill, and the teenager jumped down, but he had barely disappeared through the scrub oaks when McConnell found himself staring at the business end of a sawed-off shotgun.

To McConnell's further amazement, the masked intruder knew Jimmy had gotten off the stage and also evidently knew the strongbox was bolted to the floor of the coach because he told McConnell to unhitch the horses and take them several yards out of sight of the vehicle. McConnell could still hear the ring of a hatchet breaking into the strongbox as Jimmy emerged from behind the ridge to rejoin the stage, as previously agreed. The pair crept back over the hilltop and saw the robber back out of the coach holding a gold-filled sack. Passing Jimmy's gun back and forth

Following his encounter with Black Bart, stage driver Reason McConnell embarked on a successful career as a shotgun messenger for Wells Fargo & Company. *Author's collection.*

between them, both fired but missed, and the robber vanished into a thick stand of manzanita. At Copperopolis, they reported the holdup to Sheriff Ben Thorn, who quickly reasoned that the culprit had to have been on higher ground than the robbery site to have seen Jimmy leave the stage. The trio returned to the area, where Sheriff Thorn spotted a great boulder near the crest of the hilltop. Behind the boulder, Thorn found, among other items, a sack containing a pound of sugar and a few crackers, and a linen handkerchief with a laundry mark in one corner.

The laundry mark was laboriously traced to a Mr. C.E. Bolton, who lived in a rented room at the Webb House in San Francisco. After securing a search warrant, the police discovered all the evidence they needed to arrest the dapper, white-haired "mining investor" who had been christened Charles E. Bowles in 1829, changing the spelling to "Boles" during the years he served as a Union army sergeant in the Civil War. After hours of denial, Bolton/Boles/Bowles finally consented to tell where he had buried the Funk Hill holdup treasure if Wells Fargo agreed not to press charges on the other twenty-seven successful holdups. Authorities agreed—but how had he known that the strongbox would be bolted to the stagecoach floor? The affable, cultured gentleman had spent a few days in Tuttletown "making friends" with the shippers, that's how. Sentenced in 1883 to six years in San Quentin, the West's most colorful stage robber was released for good behavior in 1888 and then quietly vanished…while his legend grew larger every passing decade.

THE RUGGLES BROTHERS

Charles Bowles's stage holdup days ended with at least a modicum of dignity. Violence marked the passing of Charles and John Ruggles, two troubled brothers hard up for cash who decided to rob the Weaverville stage en route to Shasta in May 1892. Johnny Boyce was driving when two masked figures emerged from the surrounding chaparral thickets. To the brothers' disgust, the take was small. They picked a spot on the same route closer to Redding, and a few days later, Charley Ruggles jumped from behind a clump of low oaks, yelling for the stage to halt.

Johnny Boyce was again on the box, only this time he carried some $3,300 escorted by messenger Amos "Buck" Montgomery, a well-liked and respected man. Boyce threw out the strongbox as ordered, but something rattled Charley, and in minutes rapid gunfire was exchanged. Boyce was wounded in both legs, his other passenger was shot in one leg, Montgomery was bleeding from multiple gun wounds and robber Charley Ruggles took shots to his head and face. Controlling the frightened horses as best he could, Boyce made a dash for it—but not before John Ruggles leaped from his hiding place to shoot Montgomery in the back. Charley was captured the next day; John Ruggles was arrested a month later in Woodland. Both were held in the Redding jail to await trial.

Then rumors began circulating that the Ruggleses' defense attorney was planning to implicate the murdered Buck Montgomery in the crime.

Look Out for Stage Robber and Murderer!

$1100 REWARD

For the Arrest and Conviction of

JOHN D. RUGGLES,

Who was principally concerned in the robbing of the stage near Redding, May 14th, and the murder of Messenger Montgomery.

DESCRIPTION.

He is thirty-two years of age; 5 feet 11½ inches high, weight 175 pounds; born in California; light or florid complexion, long features; heavy, light brown moustache (now colored black), light brown hair, dark blue eyes; long features, high forehead, square chin; wears number 8 or 9 shoes and 7¼ hat; when last seen wore a black felt hat; has large scar on right side of neck caused by burn; has large brown mole below shoulder-blade; scar on breast-bone; gunshot wound on leg; large, bony hands, calloused from work; restless and uneasy, looking around out of corners of eyes, looking sharply right and left when talking to you; most always has mouth open; smokes cigarettes and makes them; has a habit of clearing his throat every little while, caused by being an inveterate cigarette smoker; does not drink to any extent; folds his arms across his breast when talking to any one, and generally standing or leaning against something; at time of robbery wore a dark coat, spring-bottom bluish pants, with welt-seam along the sides; he carried two 44 cal. Colt bronze pistols.

He was sent to San Quentin November 16th, 1878, from San Joaquin County, for a term of seven years, for robbery, and was pardoned and restored to citizenship February 26th, 1880.

He lived many years with his parents near Woodland, Yolo County. He owns a quarter section of improved land in Tulare County, near Traver, mortgaged to the Sacramento Bank for $4,500, and is well known in that county. For two or three years past has spent considerable time, summers, hunting in Shasta and Siskiyou Counties, and is proficient in the use of all kinds of firearms. He is an extraordinary footman, and can outtravel a horse on mountains; is a thorough mountaineer.

In the robbery, 14th instant, he took from the Express Box 79½ ozs. of quicksilvered gold from Weaverville, about 880 fine, and valued at $1,300; also, 96½ ozs. gold amalgam, about 730 fine, and valued at $1,400; also about $675 in coin. Total, $3,375.

In addition to the $600 standing reward offered by the State and Wells, Fargo & Company for the arrest and conviction of this class of offenders, Governor Markham has offered $500. If arrested, wire Sheriff Green, Redding, Shasta County, Cal., or the undersigned. His conviction certain.

J. B. HUME,
J. N. THACKER,
SPECIAL OFFICERS WELLS, FARGO & Co.

SAN FRANCISCO, CAL., May 21, 1892.

Wanted poster for John Ruggles. *Author's collection.*

As a news story later described the events, "Something was in the air" in Redding on Saturday, July 23. At one o'clock the next morning, an armed force of about forty masked citizens silently entered the jail, secured the keys and marched the prisoners to a crossbeam suspended from two pine trees. Passengers on the early train could see the Ruggles brothers from their car windows, dangling from ropes in the morning sun.

TWENTIETH-CENTURY DESPERADOS

Twenty or more stage holdups occurred in northern California in the opening decades of the twentieth century, reduced from an average of twenty-five per year from the 1860s to the 1880s. Many of these involved the non-injury confrontations of coaches transporting vacationers over winding,

Artist's depiction of Charles Choate's escapades, including the Foresthill stage robbery and his attempted escape from the law at Williams. *Author's collection.*

wooded back roads from railroad depots to secluded resorts in mountain or lake regions. Dozens of fearful tourists were forced to stand on the roadside with their hands raised skyward while various bandits pocketed their cash, jewelry and watches. Some highwaymen were "chivalrous," refusing to take booty from female passengers, or gallant thieves who returned watches when the victims pleaded that their timepieces had sentimental value. Less genteel offenders confiscated everything of value.

In August 1901, Charles Choate held up the Foresthill stage, gaining just $14 for his trouble. He was arrested at Williams the following February. Between there and a waiting jail cell at Colusa, Choate was badly wounded by his captors' spitting bullets when he attempted a dramatic escape. In December 1902, the Redding-Weaverville stage was stopped two miles west of Shasta City; it was the first stage holdup in Shasta County since the Ruggles brothers' episode ten years earlier. A lone masked gunman took $200 in cash from thirteen passengers aboard the Bartlett Springs stage as it neared the dividing line between Colusa and Lake Counties in July 1903—but that same year, a far more serious incident made bold-type headlines.

The roadside grave marker of Old Joe, a stage horse killed during a 1901 robbery in Foresthill. *Photo by author.*

STAGE ROBBERIES

An attempted robbery of the Ukiah-Mendocino City stage, which was carrying up to $20,000 in payroll for the large mill companies in the area, wrought terror and death in March 1903. The cash and its guard, Wells Fargo messenger O.A. Overmeyer, were inside the coach. At the first "Halt!" from a masked highwayman who jumped out from behind a tree, Overmeyer commanded driver Harry Ousley to whip up his four-horse team, whereupon the enraged bandit riddled the fleeing vehicle with rifle bullets, in the process shooting two terrified stage horses. Ousley and his wounded animals escaped under a hail of bullets, saving the treasure chest—but Overmeyer was killed outright when several missiles passed through the vehicle. The horses died from loss of blood at a halfway house farther on. Searchers with bloodhounds lost the outlaw's trail in the rain-drenched underbrush. Two years after Overmeyer's murder, a San Quentin inmate told officials that fellow inmate James W. Finley had confided in him that he, Finley, was both the Bartlett Springs stage robber and the killer of Overmeyer during the Ukiah stage holdup attempt. James Finley was a hardened, prolific criminal who was thought to be insane or at least pretended to be. In December 1905, he was sentenced to hang at Folsom Prison for an entirely different crime.

A pair of masked gunmen held up two Plumas County stages headed for Gold Lake in 1913; shots were fired, but no one was hurt. It was the first stage robbery that anyone in the district could remember.

PART V

DRIVERS AND MESSENGERS

Small staging concerns typically consisted of no more than a handful of owner-investors who performed most functions themselves, from purchasing and maintaining equipment and way stations to scheduling, promotion and personally driving stage. Their larger counterparts were structured as hierarchies, with superintendents and supervisors of varying ranks and duties who controlled operations over an extended turf in all aspects of the business: hiring hostlers, blacksmiths, teamsters, harness makers, mechanics, veterinarians and necessary field and office personnel. Staging companies and express services both employed agents, decision-makers who represented the firm in the towns and settlements they serviced. Drivers worked for stage lines; express companies hired armed messengers to escort valuable shipments from starting point to destination. The success of these enterprises depended on astute planning and substantial capital.

A select few managers and agents achieved fame in their lifetimes. Stage drivers and messengers frequently became legends.

Idolized by small boys, envied by grown men and held in awe by the ladies, the stagecoach driver was the king of his realm—passengers occupied the seat next to him only at his personal invitation. American stage drivers refused to be called "coachmen"—a term descriptive of a servile British lackey—and wouldn't accept tips for the same reason. They did accept the sobriquet "whip," taken as it was from the symbol of their profession. An alternative title sometimes used in the West was "Jehu" from the Old Testament, Kings 9:20: "and the driving is like the driving of Jehu the son of Nimshi; for he driveth furiously." To their faces, however, drivers were respectfully addressed by their names. They all loved and understood horses. The best developed extraordinary skills, were careful not to exhaust their teams with unnecessary speed on any given run and never allowed the crackling lash of a whip to touch the flesh of their animals.

Boys who displayed interest and aptitude began learning the art of reinsmanship as young as seven or eight using a mocked-up wooden rig, schooling that continued in progressive phases until the apprentice was in his high teens. In a six-horse hitch, the horses closest to the vehicle were called wheelers, the middle pair the swing span and the front pair the leaders. The three animals on the driver's right were the "off-side"; the ones to his left were the "near-side." Drivers held the separate "ribbons" of each horse between the four fingers of each corresponding hand, manipulating each rein by gathering it in with the fingers on either side of it or separating the fingers just enough to let it slip out the exact inches needed—all the while securing the handle of a whip against their right thumbs. An accomplished whip's highly dexterous hand muscles and tendons were quite strong yet exquisitely flexible, and his practiced finger movements were so subtle that even observant passengers believed that the team swerved and turned under its own intelligence while the driver did very little.

Due to the nature of their business, most drivers led roving, unsettled lives, moving from one stage line to another or shifting from place to place on the same line. Stage drivers dressed well—they could afford to—and more often than not, the handles of their whips were inlaid with rings of silver. Favorite attire included sharply creased pants, cravats, waistcoats and tailored jackets, high leather boots and long gauntlet gloves made of silk or the finest, thinnest leather. Over their clothing they wore long linen overcoats, called "dusters," to protect their wardrobes. Reverend Henry Bellows shared his awed impressions while addressing the Society of California Pioneers in 1864:

> *If I were called on to name the only aristocracy of the State, I think I should be compelled to nominate the stage-drivers, as being on the whole the most lofty, arrogant, reserved and superior class of being on the coast—that class that has inspired me with the most terror and reverence. Their blazing red cravats, a white pocket handkerchief outside, yellow gloves, their tall white hats, occasionally varied with broad brim ones, their gloomy solemnity of manner as they mount the box, have filled my soul with a deeper sentiment of the sublime, than any other single exhibition.*

Perhaps the Reverend Dr. Bellows rode with some of the silent types. Many other stage drivers were quite fond of recounting their experiences and expounding on their personal philosophies with seat companions while on the road or while lifting a glass of spirits with fascinated hangers-on at their final stop on the run. Two exceptionally skilled drivers are celebrated for stories they spun and secrets they hid.

STAGE DRIVER CHARLEY PARKHURST

Parkhurst already had a reputation as a skilled whip in Rhode Island before he came to California in the middle of the gold rush heyday. In a span of twenty-something years, Charley drove stage over various California routes and experienced his share of near-death incidents, including a bridge that collapsed moments after he had drawn his team and coach over it. It is said that after he point-blank shot two would-be stage robbers, he wasn't bothered with that particular problem anymore. Charley sipped whiskey and gambled, smoked cigars and was always pleasant and helpful to passengers—if a little reticent to indulge in idle chatter about his personal life. When arthritis of the spine and hands forced him to retire from staging, Charley settled down on a ranch property in Watsonville, where he died in late December 1879.

A furor erupted when Charley's friends, preparing the corpse for burial, discovered that "he" was a biological woman. Newspapers across the nation picked up this sensational story, and the legend of an individual who was a courageous, esteemed reinsman for forty or more years took root. Stout-bodied, homely Charley Parkhurst is mostly remembered for masquerading as a man throughout her entire adulthood so she could drive stage, one of the most physically punishing occupations of her time.

STAGE DRIVER HANK MONK

Henry "Hank" Monk started his staging career at a tender age, driving a regular run from his hometown of Waddington, New York, to Massena, twenty miles distant. He was in his twenties when he arrived in California in 1852. He first drove the Sacramento–Auburn route for Jim Birch, then the Folsom–Placerville run for Jared Crandall. In 1857, Monk began driving

Hank Monk. *Author's collection.*

between Genoa, Nevada and Placerville, working for Crandall's successors. One journalist described him as a trim built, wiry-framed man of rather small size with an "intelligent countenance" and bright, sparkling eyes. Monk drove treacherous Sierra Nevada passes for nearly twenty-five years with only two minor accidents and always arrived on time. He is celebrated, though, for the wild ride he gave Horace Greeley, the influential editor of the *New York Tribune.*

Greeley, whose self-important blustering alienated many, was touring the West in 1859. Anxious to arrive on time for a scheduled meeting in Placerville, he boarded Monk's stage at Genoa. As the coach mounted the summit, he first complained they were going too slow—then as the team plunged downward and the terror-stricken editor was bounced around like a loose ball, he yelled at Monk to slow down. "Keep your seat, Horace," said Monk. "I'll get you there on time." Ten hours later, Mr. Greeley indeed arrived on time, shaken and bruised. His published account of the trip told of riding along "mere shelves" between yawning precipices at the breakneck speed of four California horses "so wild it took two men to harness them."

Monk was an irrepressible yarn-spinner who could hang an entire tale from a single thread; certainly, Greeley hotly denied that any part of the conversational repartee in Monk's story was true. Nonetheless, the tale took on a life of its own even before the works of Mark Twain, humorist Artemus Ward and California poet-playwright Joaquin Miller spread it—and Hank's name—far and wide. In 1866, Congressman Calvin Hulburd read Artemus Ward's satirical version on the floor of the House of Representatives to ridicule his political nemesis Horace Greeley. The whole business infuriated and humiliated Greeley, who died in 1872 in the midst of his campaign for the presidency of the United States.

It made Hank Monk a star. Articles likening this or that driver to "the famous whip Hank Monk" abounded. His personal activities and daredevil driving exploits, infrequent illnesses and witticisms regularly appeared in the pages of an adoring press. Monk received a superb $500 watch from fans in Carson City in 1863. On New Year's Day 1876, he was gifted with a complete new wardrobe by flume works employees for his past kindnesses. People chuckled when Hank jested with a Lake Tahoe tourist that he was having her unwieldy wardrobe trunk sawn in half so he could deliver it (the lady was not amused). When a newsman inquired about thawing winter conditions in the Sierra, Hank quipped that it wasn't so cold as reported, but if a man spit in the morning, the spittle reached the ground as round as a bullet and rolled off like a marble. Monk's most audacious fabrication was gleefully reported by the *Daily Alta California* in November 1864:

> *A nervous old gentleman* [was] *crossing the Sierra…and everything being new to him for it was his first appearance on* any stage *in California,*

was curious to know the why and wherefore of everything, wanting detailed explanations, and distracting the attention of the "Governor" of the vehicle from his fiery team. Casting his eyes down among the mailbags in the boot…he spied a hatchet…and he tremblingly enquired the use of this indispensible tool. Knowing his man, and wishing to put a stop to his inquisitorial, leading and cross-questioning, Monk gravely replied: "Well, sir…the fact is, there have been a good many accidents occurred on this line; limbs been broken, and other injuries from the overturning of coaches, for which the Company have had to pay heavy damages; now, in order to avoid any such after-claps, when an upset occurs and passengers have legs or arms broken or are otherwise seriously injured, we end the matter by knocking them in the head with a hatchet and putting them out of their misery at once." The old gentleman looked horrified but remained speechless for the remainder of the drive.

The "Hank Monk Schottische," an arrangement for the piano, was composed in 1878. After the railroad supplanted his Carson Valley–Placerville route, Hank took tourists only as far as Lake Tahoe's eastern shore resorts. He drove the presidential carriage for visiting President Rutherford Hayes in 1880. Not yet sixty, Hank Monk died of pneumonia in Carson City on February 28, 1883. His well-attended funeral took place at the Episcopal church; two of his pallbearers were men who had been part of Horace Greeley's Placerville reception committee twenty-four years earlier. Twenty years after his death, Nevada's executive commissioner announced that the old coach Monk had driven Greeley in was to be displayed at the June 1904 World's Fair in St. Louis, along with other Monk "relics" donated by his brother. When interviewed at his Quarry Farm in Elmira, New York, Mark Twain offered this reminiscence: "That name carries me back thirty-two years—Hank Monk. I think I was present when the watch was given to Monk [but] I am only sure that I knew Monk a little. I made one trip with Monk in that old stage…I wish I could be in St. Louis next June and take one ride with his ghost."

Dozens of stage drivers were renowned during their lifetimes. Those knights of the lash still famed today include Clark "Old Chieftain" Foss, who drove sightseers to the geysers in Calistoga during the 1860s; Williamson Lyncoya Smith of Shasta; "Big John" Littlefield, who drove stage out of Sacramento for years; George Monroe, a skilled whip who drove three presidents through Yosemite; William "Curly Bill" Gerhardt, a California Stage Company driver also immortalized by Mark Twain, as well as many

Monk's Rock on the Placerville stage route. *Library of Congress, Lawrence & Houseworth Collection.*

others who expertly executed the hairpin turns of the high Sierra's Placerville and Henness Pass routes.

Stage drivers played an important part in the social and economic development of California, one and all talented reinsmen who exalted in the thrill and challenge of guiding a four or six in hand. Occasionally, they were called on to perform other services because anything could happen in a stage.

UNUSUAL INCIDENTS IN A STAGECOACH

A baby was born inside a coach bound for San Jose. The driver pulled off the road while female passengers assisted the lady. Mother and infant son survived the ordeal in good health.

THE STAGECOACH IN NORTHERN CALIFORNIA

Driver Jerry Woods saved the day in March 1869, when the Siskiyou County sheriff, who was transporting a prisoner aboard Woods's stage, fell asleep. The prisoner grabbed the sheriff's pistol and was about to shoot him when Jerry suspected something was amiss. Stopping the stage, he seized the prisoner and tied him up.

The Mokelumne Hill stage was the scene of frantic activity one day when pale smoke was seen rising from a parcel between a gentleman passenger's knees. Since the horrendous effects of nitroglycerin had recently been in the news, all occupants except one fled the coach. So did the driver, whose team bolted down a winding grade with the solitary passenger inside still clutching his smoking package. At length, the stage smashed against a bank and stopped, still intact. No explosion came. Driver and passengers cautiously crept forward to find the gentleman at the roadside, quenching the flames of his liquids. He was a photographer, and the chemicals of his trade had caught fire.

In September 1852, a stage driver's advice even thwarted an improper romance when high in the mountain town of Weaverville, a charming young girl was bedazzled by a wily rogue and planned to run away with him. Her father, accidently learning the facts and anxious to save his daughter, spirited her to Shasta City. There the two boarded a Hall & Crandall stage for Sacramento, where they could book passage on a riverboat to San Francisco Bay. En route, a bar keeper at Hall's Hotel, who was sympathetic to the scoundrel's designs, told the coach driver a fanciful romantic tale and gave him a note to secretly pass to the girl at the first opportunity. Aware that the young lady was clearly suffering from emotional duress, he gave the girl the note, gratified that it seemed to lift her spirits.

But later that same evening over supper the driver, to his considerable dismay, learned the identity of her suitor from remarks he overheard from the other passengers. The *Sacramento Daily Union*'s account, which scornfully described the girl's would-be seducer as "a desperado, old and ungainly in appearance," didn't print his full name yet gave enough details for any reader to identify him as none other than the notorious Joseph McGee, a tax collector for Trinity County. Just three weeks prior to the planned elopement, McGee had been arrested—after first fleeing the scene—for shooting and wounding two men in a local saloon, narrowly escaping the hangman's noose at Weaverville through the intercession of a few influential friends. The chastened stage driver hastily drew the father aside, apologized for his active part in the scheme and advised him to stay over a day when the stage reached Marysville instead of continuing on the through schedule to Sacramento. This prudent course avoided a probable fatal confrontation, as the father had sworn to die before relinquishing his child, and McGee was equally determined to recapture the young lady at all costs. The scoundrel was armed and waiting for her in Sacramento on the day she should have arrived—just as his note had said. Passing through town the following day, the father safely delivered his daughter into the care of a college of nuns in San Jose, as he had intended. The ultimate fate of Joseph McGee is unknown.

SHOTGUN MESSENGERS

Stage drivers were responsible for the vehicle and team owned by their employers and for the safety of their passengers; they were not expected to risk all for an express company's treasure chest they might be carrying. As the number of stage holdups escalated, express services began hiring armed guards to accompany their more valuable shipments, but these guards were not on board on every run. Wells Fargo & Company is said to be the forerunner of this practice, employing 16 proven marksmen in 1861, 35 in the early 1870s, 110 in the 1880s and 200 in 1885. Armed guards, who were also deployed on ships and trains as well as stagecoaches, were instantly dubbed "shotgun messengers" by the press for the weapon they favored.

George Hackett, the messenger who foiled Black Bart's stage holdup attempt in 1882, was hired in December 1875 to guard shipments on stages traveling between Butte, Plumas and Yuba Counties. Aged thirty-seven when he started, Hackett leaped off more than one stage to fearlessly track retreating robbers into the brush. During his first year on the job, George followed two masked men who—hoping to prevent detection—were clad only in their underwear. Hackett confiscated their outer clothing and the gold they had stolen the day before when he discovered their camp, capturing one of the undressed robbers shortly afterward. Later in the same day that he had repulsed Black Bart outside La Porte, he was injured by a shot to the face fired by yet another highwayman as the stage neared Oroville. George Hackett died peacefully on October 11, 1895. He is buried in Marysville.

Six-and-a-half-footer Mike Tovey hired on as a Wells Fargo guard in 1872, assigned to the most dangerous routes in California. In twenty-one years of high-risk service, he was wounded only twice: in 1880 during a successful stagecoach holdup and again in 1892. The latter incident claimed the life of a fifteen-year-old girl and severely wounded stage driver Babe Raggio

The monument erected in 1929 to the memory of Wells Fargo messenger Mike Tovey at the site of his 1893 murder. *Photo by author.*

when a highwayman opened fire without warning. Tovey caught Raggio as he was falling forward, took the reins and transported the dead and stricken to a nearby ranch. Nothing was taken from the stage, which was carrying a payroll for the Sheep Ranch mine.

90

Detail on the Mike Tovey monument plaque. *Photo by author.*

Justly reputed as a fierce gunman when confronted by road agents, Tovey was in the habit of removing and pocketing his gun's ammunition over those portions of a route considered the least likely to encounter trouble. It was at just such a place that he was murdered as he sat next to driver Clint Radcliffe on June 15, 1893, on the afternoon stage from Ione to Jackson. Rifle shots cracked out from behind a stone fence as the stage ascended a grade, killing Tovey instantly. Radcliffe sustained minor injuries; two more shots crippled a horse in the leg. No one on the stage returned fire, although Clint Radcliffe glimpsed the daring ambusher from three hundred yards away. Radcliffe, a male passenger, and workers who rushed to the scene from a nearby open field lifted Tovey's body inside the coach, which limped into Jackson. Mike Tovey was widely mourned; despite suspicions and a thorough manhunt, his assassin was never found.

PART VI

ROUTES, TOWNS AND STAGE STOPS

The gold-rushing Forty-Eighters, a less publicized crowd than the subsequent stampede of those who arrived in 1849, had limited transportation choices. California had just two navigable rivers: the Sacramento and the San Joaquin. Consequently, San Francisco and river-adjacent villages were transformed into major outfitting, transportation and trading towns. When the first shiploads of fevered fortune-seekers from the east debarked at the port of San Francisco in March 1849, the *Weekly Alta California* offered this advice:

> *It is very difficult to give a good opinion as to which is the best locality for digging…and parties will be enabled to obtain more accurate information at Sacramento and Stockton for their guidance. Parties going to dig, and not to trade, should be careful not to overburden themselves with baggage. Large quantities of clothing…should not be taken, as it is difficult to procure transportation for it. There are two methods of transportation—one by land, on horseback, via San Jose and Benecia to Sacramento, and the other by a launch to Sacramento or Stockton. The difficulty of procuring horses at San Francisco renders the route by water the most feasible. On arriving at [these two cities] teams can be procured to convey provisions…to any desirable point, or perhaps two horses or mules can be purchased, one of which can be rode and the other* packed. *This last is the preferable method to one who understands the management of horses; but the novice will save himself much vexation by going on foot and sending his baggage in a wagon.*

THE STAGECOACH IN NORTHERN CALIFORNIA

Those coming overland began arriving in August and September, about the same time stagecoaching began. Miners fanned out over an extensive area; there was plenty of the precious metal in the four hundred linear miles of mountainous terrain from just south of Stockton to the Oregon border. Reports that someone had struck it rich spread rapidly, and each new discovery site, no matter how remote, attracted thousands. Merchants followed, and so did the stagecoach. The northwest corner of Sierra County was first prospected in the spring of 1850; three summers later, two enterprising entrepreneurs placed this advertisement in the *Marysville Daily Herald*:

> **STAGE HOUSE!!** *THE AMERICAN HOUSE, Situated on the Road to Sear's Diggings, fifty-four miles from Marysville. This popular house is entirely new and furnished with good clean new bedding, entirely free from bed bugs and fleas. The above house is the headquarters of all the stages on the road; in fact mule navigation commences from this place. No effort will be spared by the proprietors to keep the reputation, as it now stands, the first on the road. The best of wines, liquors, and cigars always on hand. WHITING & DRUM.*

The stagecoach eventually rolled into every city and mining town in northern California, traveling night and day "in season" through heat

A stagecoach nearing its destination. *Author's collection.*

and fog and drizzle—but not in severe winter weather, when conditions posed significant risk. Stage proprietors suspended their schedules during the months when heavy rains sliced gullies across roads, flatland plains flooded, creeks rose, landslides threatened and snow blocked upland passes. The climate and topography of the route plus the time needed to repair roads determined the duration of suspended service, on occasion lasting for months. Newspapers informed the public when regular lines ceased running in winter weather and when they resumed operations in the spring.

Coloma and Mormon Island

Still famed as the original gold discovery sites in California, Coloma and Mormon Island were the first destinations of pioneer stageman James Birch from his headquarters at the Sacramento riverfront. He left town by the Coloma Road, hardly more than a well-beaten trail clogged with gold rushers when he began wheeling his vehicles east past Sutter's Fort.

John Sutter was the agent of both momentous gold discoveries although the actual discoverer of neither. Proprietor of the only trading post and agricultural domain in the Sacramento Valley, Sutter had grand improvement plans that included a sawmill for board lumber and a larger gristmill. In the summer of 1847, a contingent of Mormon Battalion soldiers discharged from service in the Mexican-American War who were on their way home to Utah, camped outside his compound. Many were skilled mechanics, and Sutter immediately hired up to sixty of them for his many projects. The majority agreed to construct a gristmill six miles east on the American River, and six signed on as crew for Sutter's associate, James Marshall, an experienced millwright, to erect a sawmill in a timber-rich little foothills valley called Coloma.

On the morning of January 24, 1848, James Marshall picked up a few shiny flakes from the bottom of the mill's tailrace, unwittingly touching off the great California gold rush. Crew member Henry Bigler relayed the news to his Mormon Battalion comrades, who were working on Sutter's gristmill downstream, and in late February, three of them came up to see for themselves. They departed a few days later and, on their way back downhill, found gold lying close to the surface on a gravel bar in the American River. However, these men were more interested in returning to their families in Utah and didn't stake claims. The locale did not become

Looking down from the upper veranda of the Cary House, which was the stage depot on Placerville's Main Street. *Library of Congress, Lawrence & Houseworth Collection.*

a mining camp until the first week in April, when other battalion veterans, as well as a number of Mormons who had arrived by sea two years earlier, found it again. Named for the faith of its founders and the fact that mining ditches turned the gravel bar into an island, Mormon Island was one of the richest strikes in northern California.

By May, both camps were teeming with hundreds of prospectors living in tents and shanties; by early 1850, both were full-fledged towns with mercantiles, saloons, hotels, restaurants and homes. Birch's "express and daily accommodation stage lines" stopped at the St. Louis Exchange Hotel and Bailey & Winter's Hotel in Coloma. For a short time in the spring of 1852, R. Patterson & Company operated four-horse stages between Sacramento, Mormon Island, Coloma and Placerville.

For a few months in 1851, Major William Ormsby, a gold rusher who had been active on Sacramento civic committees while residing there, owned the

Coloma and Placerville line of mail stages and commenced improvements on the sinuous, rutted road. After moving to the Carson Valley around 1857, he was an agent for the Pioneer Stage Line and an early advocate of the Johnson Pass wagon road.

Coloma developed into a commercial and recreational center for the remote mining camps; fifteen miles downstream, Mormon Island served as a trading center for its own neighboring claim sites. Coloma's placer deposits were exhausted early, and by the mid-1860s, most of its fewer than 900 permanent residents had moved on. Mormon Island, which supported 2,500 souls in its heyday, gradually decreased in importance after the Sacramento Valley Railroad yards directed commercial interests toward Folsom. This notice appeared in the *Sacramento Daily Union* on June 1, 1857:

> **Completion of the Wire Suspension Bridge**. *Folsom, May 31st—6 P.M. Kinsey & Thompson have just put in crossing order their new wire suspension bridge over the American River at this place. This morning all the Auburn, Yankee Jim's and Nevada [City] stages belonging to the California Stage Company crossed it, instead of crossing Shaw's bridge at Mormon Island, which route is about three miles longer than by the new bridge.*

During the 1860s and 1870s, farms and orchards supplanted the once-bustling town square, although the name "Mormon Island" survived as a district designation until 1955, when it was submerged beneath the lake created by the Folsom Dam. Today, Coloma is a ranching and farming community and the site of James Marshall Gold Discovery State Historic Park.

Stockton

German-born Charles Weber arrived in California six years before the gold discovery. Greatly impressed by the landscape around the San Joaquin River, he acquired a Mexican land grant in excess of forty-eight thousand acres, but his efforts to colonize his land were unsuccessful until the fall of 1847, when a few settlers founded a tiny hamlet named Tuleberg. In the spring of 1848, when hundreds were passing through Tuleberg on their way to newly discovered gold mines at Angel's Camp, Jamestown and Murphy's Camp, Weber—who had established himself as a merchant in San Jose—saw the

Stockton as seen from the courthouse, 1860s. *Library of Congress, Lawrence & Houseworth Collection.*

opportunity to both further develop his property and become a local supplier. He erected a large mercantile establishment where Main and Center Streets later intersected and renamed his fledgling community for a man he greatly admired: Commodore Robert Stockton.

Located fifty miles east of the San Joaquin River, Stockton was laced with a number of tributaries and channels with high, perpendicular banks that allowed ships to easily enter the settlement. From inception, Stockton was a river port city and a major supply center to the southern mines. The first ferry was established in April 1849 on the San Joaquin River at the old crossing along the land route from Sacramento to San Jose and Oakland. By July, Stockton had expanded from a village of fifty residents to a town of one thousand.

Wagons and mule teams relayed freight into the mining camps; men walked or rode until Maurison founded a stage service in June 1849, leaving

Stockton every other day for the Stanislaus River mines, a journey that took twelve hours. Maurison's service was apparently brief, leaving a gap in staging services until 1850, when merchant Joshua Holden, hauling his own goods, noticed many travelers walking to the mines and decided to carry passengers. One of the first gold miners in Sonora and a large landowner in both Stockton and Sonora, Holden founded a daily line of stages between the two towns, equipped his line with quality stage horses and acquired "comfortable stages," as one lady passenger enthused. A year later, he sold out to Kelley, Reynolds & Company. In February 1851, two Frenchmen, Guibal and Dhorboure, established a tri-weekly stage line to run between Stockton and Mokelumne Hill, but in less than a month they encountered competition for the same route from another staging firm owned by Frenchmen Provinde and Paxon. The latter left Stockton on Tuesdays and Thursdays at 7:30 a.m. and left "The Hill" on Wednesdays and Sundays at 3:00 p.m. Their fare was twelve dollars.

Mokelumne Hill in the 1860s. *Library of Congress, Lawrence & Houseworth Collection.*

Alonzo McCloud started a stage line to Sonora in 1852, making a record time of six hours back to Stockton in a daring drive on August 18, 1853, to bring news of a fire that was raging in Sonora when he had left it at two o'clock in the morning. In 1854, the Fisher brothers Alvin and Samuel purchased McCloud's line. They put on a daily line of stages, equipped their lines with fine horses and Concord coaches, carried mail and passengers to all the mountain camps and occupied the former El Dorado gambling house on the corner of Levee and Center Streets as a staging office. By the end of the year, the Fisher brothers' chief competition was the California Stage Company.

After selling his stage lines to the Fishers, Alonzo McCloud's second staging endeavor, a daily line between Stockton and Oakland, was a response to Stocktonians' growing feelings that they were being price-gouged by steamship lines. His stages left the Weber House at one o'clock in the afternoon; at Alviso, passengers boarded a ferry for San Francisco. In retaliation, the monopolistic California Steam Navigation Company reduced its fares, forcing the stage line out of business. The steamship line triumphed again after a second attempt in August 1859.

There was competition and opposition on the Stockton–Sacramento stage route as well. Stage service between the two cities was inaugurated from Sacramento in late 1850 but later abandoned due to road conditions until May 1851, when James Birch established his Tri-Weekly Line of stages to Stockton (later absorbed into the California Stage Company). There were two stage roads: the Upper Sacramento Road, which crossed at Staples Ferry on the Mokelumne River, and the Lower Sacramento Road that skirted the tule lands past Woodbridge. Both were terrible winter roads that were not improved until 1863, six years before the railroad arrived at Stockton. The leading driver on the Lower Road was "Peg-Leg" Johnny Smith, one of several who expertly piloted their teams and coaches through immense swamps. Stages going to and from Sacramento and Stockton on the Upper Sacramento Road stopped for meals at Staples' ranch.

SACRAMENTO

Sacramento sprang to life as a trading village on the banks of the Sacramento River, essentially created by merchants who wanted to capitalize on the hordes of gold seekers coming inland from San Francisco's seaport. It was an

A two-story inn and stage stop on the Sacramento–Folsom road in 1852, Mills Station has since endured relocations, reconstructions and changing uses. *Photo by author.*

important river port even before the town itself was surveyed and mapped in December 1848.

By late 1851, several separate stage lines were coming and going daily from staging offices at the Crescent City and Missouri Hotels. Stagemen headquartered in Sacramento—many of whom owned several vehicles running over multiple routes—included James Birch, William Beeks and Slocum & Morse. Munroe & Company provided stage service to Shasta City, changing the southern terminus of its line to Colusa in October.

On August 27, 1851, the *Sacramento Daily Union* commented:

> *A beautiful and elegant stage coach made its appearance in our streets yesterday, driven by that pioneer stager, Birch. As it passed our office, with six splendidly caparisoned horses, we were strongly reminded of "days lang syne."*

The following year, Cartwright, Swain & Company established lines leaving Sacramento for the mines on the Mokelumne River by way of Ione Valley.

Coover & Woodward opened a daily line of mail stages bound for Drytown, Jackson and Mokelumne Hill and intermediate points. Rosencrants & Cutts provided four-horse stages to Auburn and vicinity. Patterson & Company, bound for Mormon Island, Coloma and Placerville, left the Missouri and Harp Hotels at seven o'clock every morning, advertising "through to Coloma and Placerville in seven hours!" Charles Green's Concord coaches departed the Orleans Hotel for Auburn. Haworth & Swift, the buyer of James Birch's Telegraph Line, left Sacramento at 7:00 a.m. and passed through Wheatland, Rough and Ready and Grass Valley before arriving in Nevada City at 5:00 p.m. the same day, including Sundays.

James Birch ran stages from Sacramento to Nicolaus and Marysville; J. Smith offered a four-horse mail line to Stockton, a through trip of eight hours each way. In June 1852, Hall & Crandall established stage service from Sacramento to Shasta City, and in early 1853, Charles Green—who became a prominent independent stage operator—announced the creation of his Forrest Line from Sacramento to Sonora but sold this line to M.H. McCormick in 1856.

Stages seldom departed Sacramento without as many passengers as the vehicle would hold. Always cognizant of the value of the Sacramento River as the "highway" to the coast, stage proprietors invariably inserted phrases in their advertisements to the effect that their stages arrived at Sacramento in time to connect with the steamships for San Francisco.

All this staging activity provided steady employment for drivers, staging agents, stable owners, relay station keepers and a variety of mechanics and artisans, as well as increased business for hotels and restaurants. Freight wagons rumbled in and out of town daily, many of them owned by staging concerns. The agents and clerks of more than a dozen express agencies were kept busy night and day loading and unloading their strongboxes from the vehicles of the staging companies they used to transport their shipments. Adams & Company, the dominant express service until 1855, owned an impressive building on Second Street. Well Fargo & Company moved in at number 11 J Street, between Front and Second.

Sacramento became the state capital in 1854 and by the end of 1855 had become the largest stagecoaching center in the nation, a distinction it held for another decade despite the opening, in February 1856, of the Sacramento Valley Railroad, a 22-mile rail line between Sacramento and Folsom. Within a few months, several stage companies and freighters relocated their headquarters to Folsom, Placerville, Auburn and elsewhere, but California Stage Company coaches still departed daily from the city. By 1861—when

Sacramento reenacts its past during annual Gold Rush Days. *Photo by Sally Myers, Tom Myers Photography.*

the *Union*'s editors reflected that the staging business was poor in comparison with former years—nine independent lines had entered the field, for a grand total of 1,557 miles of staging carried on between Sacramento and other portions of the state and adjacent regions.

In May 1856, the California Stage Company's new president, James Haworth, relocated company headquarters, and his family, to Marysville, a move that did not diminish extensive and profitable operations out of Sacramento. The stage company's stables and storage facilities on E Street between Eleventh and Twelfth, leased from another party, burned to the ground on April 1, 1857. The fire originated in a frame building filled with baled hay, spreading to an adjoining structure that housed fifty-five stagecoaches and wagons. The cause of the fire was generally thought to be arson.

Auburn

California residents were already hurrying into the foothills to prospect the gold found at Sutter's sawmill in Coloma when French-born Claude Chana, a cooper in the sometime employ of John Sutter, set out for the site with a party of friends. Led by an experienced mountain man, the group rode southeast from Chana's home on the Bear River over unexplored country. On May 16, 1848, Chana discovered gold in a dry ravine some twenty miles from their destination. The group hastily set up camp and began mining.

First known as North Fork Dry Diggings, the camp was renamed Wood's Dry Diggings after John S. Wood built a log cabin and settled. The lack of water was a hindrance to gold panning in the dry months, which resulted in a sparse population at first, until the wet season returned to fill the creeks. The location, however, was prime. Roughly centered between the developing gold rush towns of Marysville, Sacramento, Nevada City, Placerville and the extensive Foresthill mining districts, Dry Diggings began attracting a larger population after William Gwynn and H.M. House opened trading posts. The village was officially named Auburn in late 1849. By 1850, framed, painted structures were replacing the earlier tents and cloth houses of a populace now swelled to more than 1,300. Named the Placer County seat in 1851, Auburn developed into a trading and supply point of considerable

The Auburn stage, 1860s or later. This one is a mud wagon with a canvas top and open siding. *Author's collection.*

importance in the region, the hub of an ever-expanding system of wagon roads, ferries and bridges radiating in all directions.

In September 1852, the *Placer Herald* noted that several stages arriving and departing daily were doing a flourishing business: three for Sacramento, one for Marysville, one for Grass Valley and Nevada City, one for Yankee Jim's and one for Illinoistown (Colfax). The following year, a correspondent to the *Sacramento Daily Union* reported, "We now have a daily line of stages to Coloma and Hangtown (Placerville), making a continued line from Sonora in the southern, to Shasta and Downieville in the northern mines." Passengers boarded and departed coaches at the Empire and National Hotels.

Several more stage lines serving Auburn and environs appeared over the following decades, still providing transportation and mail delivery to the remote mining districts after the Central Pacific Railroad came through town in 1865. Perhaps the last new stage line was the twice-daily stage service between Sacramento and Auburn established by Charles Z. Brockway in July 1894, passing through Antelope, Roseville, Rocklin, Loomis, Penryn and Newcastle. In December 1896, the Auburn stage to Georgetown was held up on a lonely wooded road, a relatively uncommon crime in that decade. But forty years earlier, a stage stop seven miles below Auburn had been the scene of considerable villainous activity.

THE MOUNTAINEER HOUSE

In its day, this well-known hostelry and tavern set on semi-wooded ranch land was the only stage station on the busy road between Folsom and Auburn where the coaches of the California Stage Company and other lines changed their teams. Horses and equipment were housed in a barn described as the largest in the county; stagecoaches and stable hands came and went daily. Other travelers delivering wagonloads of goods passed by on the dusty road, too, often stopping in for liquid refreshment.

The Mountaineer House was also a thieves' hideout and rendezvous.

Jack Phillips, an Englishman, and "Sydney Duck" (a former inmate of the Australian penal colony), owned the establishment. No evidence exists of the exact date the roadhouse first came into existence, but it is likely that Phillips was the first owner of the property and the person who constructed the inn, a two-story structure measuring thirty by forty feet with a bar and

A cut-stone fence is all that remains of the infamous Mountaineer House tavern and stage stop. *Photo by author.*

dining room downstairs. Upstairs served as the family's quarters, with spaces allotted for overnight guests.

Phillips advertised the property for sale "very low" in early 1852, apparently unsuccessfully because he was still the proprietor four years later when he gave sanctuary to a local horse thief named Richard Barter, better known as "Rattlesnake Dick." That same spring and summer, Jack Phillips aided and abetted the notorious Tom Bell and his motley gang, who were soon to go on record as the first outlaws to hold up a California stage. Bell and his associates frequently met at the Mountaineer House between lawless sprees, where they could camp and hide in a ravine a distance beyond the tavern. Phillips "spotted" for the gang, tipping them off when a traveler carrying a fat purse happened by so they could follow and rob him a few miles down the road.

Acting on such a tip in June, the Bell gang followed Samuel Rosenthal on his way from Grass Valley to Folsom. Engaging the victim in distracting conversation that turned ugly, Bell and his accomplices tied Rosenthal to a tree in the surrounding woods, took the $1,250 they found in his clothing and left him to die—but remembered to ride back some days later to the

Mountaineer House to give Jack Phillips his share of $150. After his arrest for the August 1856 Camptonville stage holdup, Bell's second in command, Bill Gristy, volunteered that Bell himself had "probably" sneaked back to murder Rosenthal after the others had left the scene. A month after the Bell gang members were either dead or in custody, a couple out for an evening stroll discovered animal-scattered bones under a pine tree. Rosenthal's remains were identified by his boots.

Hoping to save himself from an extended prison term for his part in the Camptonville stage holdup and other crimes, Bill Gristy quickly told all about his fellow thugs—including Jack Phillips. "This house is a stage house," Bill Gristy told his interrogators, "and all the hostlers and every person around it knew us and our business." On October 2, 1856, the *Sacramento Daily Union* reported the innkeeper's inevitable fate:

> *ARREST OF A SUPPOSED ROBBER.—On Monday, Sept. 29th, Jack Phillips, proprietor of the Mountaineer House, on the Auburn Road, was arrested by the Sheriff of Stanislaus County, assisted by some citizens of Placer County. He had been implicated in some of the recent robberies committed in that neighborhood, by one of the highwaymen lately captured at Knights Ferry in Stanislaus County.*

Allegedly, Jack Phillips was the mastermind behind the bandits' inter-gang identification: a marked bullet with a hole bored through it and suspended from a knotted string. Other innkeepers such as Mrs. Elizabeth Hood, proprietress of the Western Exchange Hotel on the road to Nevada City, and Mrs. Cole and John Gardiner, who owned the California House twenty-five miles from Marysville, were also willing accomplices in Tom Bell's activities. If a stranger pulled this oddity from his pocket when paying for a meal or drink, he was recognized as one of the ring.

A month prior to his trial in Auburn on February 19, 1857, when he was sentenced to two years in San Quentin, Phillips sold the Mountaineer House to Henry William Hook. In July 1857, the road between Auburn and the Mountaineer House became part of the Auburn Ravine Turnpike toll road, whereupon Mr. Hook put the property on the market, placing weekly advertisements like this one that appeared in the *Sacramento Daily Union* on July 30, 1857:

> *TAVERN STAND AND RANCH FOR SALE—The undersigned offers for sale the valuable and well known Ranch and Tavern Stand known as*

the MOUNTAINEER HOUSE, six miles below Auburn and 12 miles from Folsom, on the old Sacramento Road, being the only Stage station between those points. The Ranch contains 160 acres, 100 of which is fenced and under cultivation. There is also a lot of Stock on the premises. All the above will be sold low, if applied for soon. Terms cash. H.W. HOOK, Mountaineer house.

A subsequent owner increased the acreage and constructed a granite-block ranch house on the foundations of the original inn after it burned to the ground in 1860.

YANKEE JIM'S

In 1850, a horse thief calling himself Yankee Jim discovered gold on a ridge between the North and Middle Forks of the American River, eighteen miles northeast of Auburn and about three miles northwest of the already active gold camps at Foresthill. According to legend, the thief built a corral for his stolen horses atop the richest mine in the vicinity, but miners from the Foresthill camps heard rumors about the quality of his find and rushed in, discovered his criminal activities and ran him off under threat of an immediate lynching.

Nonetheless, they named the new settlement Yankee Jim's. The camp was characterized as a "dry diggings" until the early summer of 1852, when enterprising mining companies succeeded in completing an elaborate system of canals, ditches and flumes to carry water from Shirt Tail Canyon. Some 1,300 feet higher than Auburn, from inception the camp was considered almost inaccessible except to mules and pedestrians, but narrow trails were soon widened into wagon roads, and the growing numbers of residents were elated to learn, in late April 1852, that they would soon have stage service between themselves and Sacramento as soon as a bridge then in progress over the North Fork was completed. On May 13, 1852, Frank Brown and William Parish, who had purchased the mail line and equipment of Rosecrans & Cutts, commenced service to Yankee Jim's from Sacramento via Auburn with a "Splendid Four Horse Daily Line of Mail Stages." Two weeks later, Charles Green's People's Opposition Line (to the mail service) announced a second service:

Yankee Jim's Road is the old 1850s stage road still in use today for automobiles between Foresthill, Yankee Jim's and Colfax. *Photo by author.*

SPLENDID CONCORD STAGE COACHES FOR OPHIR! AUBURN! and YANKEE JIM'S DIGGINGS! Departing daily from Sacramento at 7:00 A.M., stopping at all the Bars, Gulches, Canons, and Bluffs on the Middle and South Forks of the American River, arriving at Yankee Jim's Diggings at 4 o'clock P.M. same day. Returning, will leave Hunter & Company's Express Office, Yankee Jim's Diggings, every morning at 4 o'clock, passing through, by and near [the above places], *and arriving at Sacramento City in season to dine and connect with the steamers for San Francisco same day.*

The bonanza came the next year after severe storms in the winter of 1852–53 caused a huge landslide, exposing an abundance of gold at the head of Jenny Lind Canyon that yielded $2,000 to $2,500 every day. Colonel William McClure introduced hydraulic mining operations in 1853, a method Yankee Jim's was known for through the 1870s, as the Jenny Lind mine produced a total output of $1.1 million. As an individual stage proprietor, James Birch serviced Yankee Jim's, and his California Stage Company coaches rolled regularly into town from September 1854 forward.

The "new" Yankee Jim's Road Bridge built in 1929. *Photo by author.*

At one time, five thousand people resided in Yankee Jim's (where the town site was located and still stands, not the gulch known to the pioneers as "Yankee Jim's Dry Diggings"). It was a rowdy village noted for murderous mayhem in its saloons, a no-nonsense vigilance committee and the Indian Queen, a house of ill repute. In four years, it matured into an important town, replete with flourishing hotels, shops of all descriptions, churches, schools and outlying ranches. Today, few call it home.

Yankee Jim's Road is the old stagecoach road between Colfax and Foresthill, a narrow, pothole-ridden lane of dirt-covered bedrock with hairpin turns and a 1,000-foot drop on the outer edge. Notices of current gold claims are tacked to tree trunks here and there along its length, and the remnants of old orchards can be glimpsed between the pines. The route now traverses a twentieth-century, one-lane suspension bridge that spans a 204-foot chasm across the North Fork of the American River.

MARYSVILLE

Flood-swollen rivers in the winter of 1849–50 allowed the larger steamships from San Francisco to reach New Mecklenburg, a trading post situated within the Y formed by the confluence of the Yuba and Feather Rivers. Gold miners were already working the region's placers, having arrived via smaller watercraft at a settlement named Vernon, until then presumed to be the head of navigation on the Feather River, but this new landing on Charles Covillaud's ranch at the southern foot of what became D Street was much closer to the mining districts. Covillaud promptly surveyed a town site named in honor of his bride, Mary Murphy, a Donner Party survivor. Vernon disappeared. Marysville emerged as a major river port town, for a while the third-largest city in California after San Francisco and Sacramento.

From the settlement's earliest days, ships brought supplies, merchants and prospectors upriver to the town plaza at First and D Streets. From there, pack-mule trains and ox-drawn freight wagons were the dominant means of transportation to Long Bar, Park's Bar, Rose Bar and other camps. Strategically placed bridges and ferries enabled the stagecoach to enter town, but stage service from downriver towns attracted little patronage in 1850, when the river was high, although the Excelsior Line ran daily between Marysville and Park's Bar and Langton's Express and Passenger Line established a route to Downieville. In October of the following year, a correspondent informed the *Sacramento Daily Union* that "nine stages arrived from Sacramento today, filled to overflowing, and the travel up is fully equal to that [going] down." James Birch's Telegraph Line and Slocumb & Morse's Pilot Line served Marysville in 1851, boarding and discharging passengers at the United States Hotel.

In 1853, Hall & Crandall opened a mail stage line from Sacramento to Shasta through Marysville. Stagemen Buckingham & Adriance had three lines: Marysville to Park's Bar, Marysville to Auburn and Marysville to Nevada City. Charles McLaughlin ran stages to Downieville, Oregon House, Bidwell's Bar (today submerged beneath Lake Oroville) and Sear's Diggings. By mid-decade, the California Stage Company, Charles Green and D.F. Rogers & Company operated stages into the surrounding mining districts and between Marysville, Nevada City and Camptonville.

The California Stage Company erected large stables and a carriage house in the vicinity of A and B and First Streets in 1856. Its general stage offices were originally at Murray's Western House on the corner of Second and D Streets, where stages departed daily for Chico, Tehama, Shasta, Yreka,

Lithograph of Marysville by Kuchel & Dresel, 1856. *Courtesy California State Library, Sacramento.*

Grass Valley, Bidwell's Bar—and two stages daily to Sacramento. Two years later, the company moved its stage offices to Brumagin's Building on the east side of D near Second Street. Other stage lines departed from Barclay's National Hotel on High Street, the Philadelphia Temperance House and the St. Charles Hotel—apparently a favored name among innkeepers since many pioneer communities boasted a St. Charles Hotel or Inn.

A few miles south, a ferry service and, later, a bridge made Nicolaus an active stage stop. Eastbound stages stopped at the Empire Ranch near Smartsville, where meals were served. The well-traveled stage road between Marysville and Camptonville wound along portions of modern-day Marysville Road.

AMADOR COUNTY

Originally known as Bottileas or Botellas (bottles), apparently named for the debris scattered about by passersby, the future site of Jackson was a convenient crossing place for prospectors on their way to and from Sacramento and Stockton and the rich diggings at Mokelumne Hill. A trading post opened in 1848 near the creek; in the fall of 1849, as more gold rushers flooded in, this watercourse was named Jackson's Creek. A few miles north of Jackson, other miners named a creek and subsequent town Sutter Creek after John Sutter of Sutter's Fort and Amador City in honor of José María Amador, a native California rancher who mined there in 1848.

Drytown in Amador County, circa 1860s. *Library of Congress, Lawrence & Houseworth Collection.*

The placers in the area weren't rich, but gold was discovered in quartz rock ledges nearby in 1851, and Jackson, the logical geographic center for a large mining area, became a trade and government center for the region. That year, Jackson got a post office, stagecoach service and designation as the seat of Calaveras County, a status it retained when Amador County was created in 1854.

Leonard & Company's Stage Express commenced service from Sacramento to Drytown and Jackson in March 1851; in May, stage proprietors Culver & Rochford ran a weekly mail stage from Stockton. The following spring, Green & Marice announced a daily service from Sacramento to Drytown and Jackson, passing through all the principal places in the vicinity. Their stage depots were at the Union House, Jackson; the Buck-Eye House in Sutter Creek; the Amador House in Amador City; Rancheria House, Rancheria; and Crane's Store in Drytown. The American House in Sutter Creek, later the American Exchange Hotel, was a lively facility for stages and Adams & Company Express when the hotel opened about 1853. In November 1854, twenty-one Jackson-bound passengers reportedly left Sacramento daily in the California Stage Company's Troy-manufactured coaches.

John Vogan and Charles Green partnered in a staging business in the early 1850s, with a line of Concord and Troy coaches running from Jackson,

Iron Ivan, the last steam locomotive to operate over the Amador Central Railroad between Ione and Martell. *Photo by author.*

through Drytown, to Sacramento daily. They sold this line to the California Stage Company but shortly thereafter inaugurated another: Green's Forrest Line. Operating as Green & Vogan ten years later, they served Amador and Calaveras Counties from stages offices at Sacramento's Ebner's Hotel. After retiring from staging, John Vogan built a toll road from Ione City to Jackson. His residence, the Mountain Spring House, was a stage station.

Other notable stage stations in the region were Central House on the road between Plymouth and Drytown; Ham's Station and Cook's Station; Kirkwood Station, sixty-five miles east of Jackson, where Amador, Alpine and El Dorado Counties intersect; and the McLaughlin Ranch, known today as Volcano's Daffodil Hill.

Quartz-mining operations in Jackson, Amador City, Plymouth and Sutter Creek sustained these communities—and stage lines—for decades. Raggio Brothers established stage service between Jackson and Ione in 1882 as an additional line to their successful staging business in Calaveras County, and for many years, John Steiner ran a daily stage line between Jackson and Plymouth. John Raggio, born in California after the gold rush, managed his family's staging interests, which grew to ownership of twenty-five coaches and eighty horses. Involved in real estate, mining and logging interests, as well as staging, he was a well-known and popular figure in both counties who took an active interest in community affairs and civic improvements. He became a banker in 1904. Three years later, he was appointed the receiver of the bankrupt Ione & Eastern Railroad (renamed the Amador Central after its foreclosure sale). John Raggio died in 1921, when a new generation enthralled with mechanized transportation considered stagecoaches as part of a picturesque past.

Jackson, Amador City, Sutter Creek and Ione—the last developed as a supply center instead of a gold town—still thrive. Drytown, home to a large population and four ore-crushing stamp mills in the late 1850s, had just 167 residents according to the 2010 census.

DOWNIEVILLE AND GOODYEARS BAR

The arrival of a stagecoach always created excitement, especially in isolated communities. Miners dropped their tools and townspeople gathered because the stage brought mail, news from the outside world, returning residents, occasional new faces and even—sometimes—new females to gawk at. On

September 22, 1859, the residents of Downieville and Goodyears Bar were elated to greet the first stagecoach to reach them since the inception of their towns ten years earlier.

Over the newly completed road linking them with Camptonville rumbled Green & Company's stage, a Concord coach festooned with flags and banners drawn by four fine black horses decked out in appropriate colors. That morning, a large number of Downieville citizens accompanied by a band went to Goodyears Bar to await the stage and from there followed it back into Downieville, where driver C.E. Green drew rein at one o'clock surrounded by cheering townsfolk. Thereafter, Green & Company ran a daily stage between Downieville and Marysville, a distance of sixty-four winding miles via Goodyears Bar.

First known as The Forks for its location where the Downie River flows into the larger North Yuba, Downieville was founded in 1849 by miners roaming north in search of fresh gold fields. In February 1850, it was renamed in honor of Major William Downie, one of the first inhabitants. Brothers Miles and Andrew Goodyear established their mining camp four miles southwest

Pack mules in Downieville. *Courtesy California State Library, Sacramento.*

in the summer of 1849. The region was extremely rich in gold deposits; in the spring of 1850, upward of five thousand miners swarmed in, and both settlements prospered. By the mid-1850s, Downieville was the fifth-largest town in California and a trading center for other outlying gold camps. Sam Langston established a mule-train express service in 1850, delivering mail and other express matter from Marysville over rugged alpine trails. Wells Fargo & Company Express succeeded Langton's in 1866.

Getting there was the hard part. Downieville was nestled in a wooded amphitheater surrounded by lofty peaks. Goodyears Bar occupied a small, triangular flat in a mountain gorge. Until the stage road opened, everything from provisions to furniture had to be brought in on the backs of mules and then dragged down almost perpendicular slopes.

Stages traversing the new road cut out of the sides of mountains stopped at the Mountain House, a large hotel and stable facility perched on a summit, and the St. Charles Hotel in Goodyears Bar. The California Stage Company maintained offices in Henry's Exchange Hotel in Downieville.

THE HENNESS PASS WAGON ROAD

A year prior to the opening of the Camptonville–Downieville road, sensational news of the rich and extensive silver deposits in Nevada had caused the start of an immense reverse migration. Hundreds of miners walked out of the California gold mines and headed east, some on foot, over any road or trail available. One of these was a trail that had been used by westbound 1849 gold rushers starting from Verdi, Nevada, through the Henness Pass and over the ridge between the North and Middle Forks of the Yuba River. Traversing the entire width of Sierra County, the winding, ridge-top trail dipped south of Downieville and Goodyears Bar, circled through Forest City and Alleghany and terminated at Camptonville. In October 1859, private investors raised subscriptions to improve the trailbed as a toll road, but winter was coming, and the road—endorsed by its supporters in Sutter, Yuba, Nevada and Sierra Counties as the most direct, shortest and most practicable route to the Comstock—was not in suitable condition for heavy freight wagons until the following summer. Second only to the Placerville–Carson route, the Henness Pass Road was a primary route to the Comstock between 1860 and 1868, the year the Central Pacific Railroad's first passenger car steamed into Reno.

In July 1861, the California Stage Company began running over this route. The following year, its first daily coach from Virginia City to Marysville via Henness Pass, a distance of 130 miles, accomplished the trip in twenty-four hours. Two years hence, the company advertised daily stages from Sacramento over the Henness Pass Road to Virginia City, through in twenty-eight hours. Its competitors over portions of the route included the Nevada Stage Company and the Pacific Stage and Express Company. Toll stations and way stations included the Plum Valley House near Alleghany, owned by John Bope; the Snow Tent Hotel and stage stop; Fred's Ranch east of Forest City; and Webber's Ranch over the summit near Webber Lake.

SHASTA, SISKIYOU AND TRINITY COUNTIES

Major Pierson B. Reading was the first permanent settler in Shasta County after receiving, in 1844, the northernmost Mexican land grant awarded, nearly twenty-seven thousand acres extending twenty miles along the west bank of the Sacramento River. Reading was visiting Sutter's Fort in early 1848, when local excitement over James Marshall's gold discovery was spreading, and after visiting Coloma, he returned home to find gold on Clear Creek a few miles west of his ranch and, soon thereafter, over the ridge into Trinity County, where he mined $80,000 (in excess of $1.6 million today) in six weeks. His spectacular success immediately drew hordes of prospectors into the extreme northwestern environs.

They came south from Oregon with ox-drawn wagons and mule trains. Some sailed into fog-shrouded Humboldt Bay and walked inland through dense forests, a trek made easier after the town of Eureka developed in 1850. Seafarers landing at San Francisco took riverboats to Marysville, purchased pack mules and walked or rode 126 miles to Reading's Springs or Reading's Diggings, as the town of Shasta was first known, because the Sacramento River was impossible to navigate by steamer north of Red Bluff—and that far only when the river was seasonally high.

The tent and lean-to camp, situated at the head of wagon navigation—the point where the terrain forced northbound wagons to halt and pack-mule trains to begin—improved rapidly, boasting three hotels, dozens of houses, a large number of stores, three blacksmith shops and two ten-pin bowling alleys by mid-March 1851. A month later, a post office opened.

The Stage Driver's Memorial at Shasta State Historic Park. *Photo by author.*

The first stagecoach to arrive in Shasta came up from Sacramento in the spring of 1851, driven by Marshall McCummings. Uriah P. Munroe, who owned a ranch thirty-eight miles above Colusa, was the line's proprietor, operating as Munroe & Company (Baxter & Munroe after 1853). When the town of Colusa was founded in October 1851, Munroe took off his southern terminus at Sacramento in favor of connecting with the packet boats that sailed upriver into the new settlement, having been awarded a mail contract for the Colusa–Shasta route. Prior to this, he had laid out the town of Munroeville, a popular stage stop situated on his ranchlands.

The following April, Johnson & Company and Hall & Crandall established stage service from Colusa to Shasta, both running daily against Munroe & Company's alternate-days schedule. Hall & Crandall was authorized to carry mail to Shasta from Marysville beginning in May, sparking a lively debate over which route was faster. Hall & Crandall's depots were at the United States Hotel in Marysville and the El Dorado and Globe Hotels in Shasta City, with fourteen intermediate stops. Of the fourteen, Nicholas, Marysville, Hamilton, Bidwell's Ranch, Slawson's Ranch, Tehama and Cottonwood Creek were United States mail towns. Cole & Company stages between Colusa and Shasta commenced around the same time, reportedly well laden with passengers. Of these competing lines, Johnson & Company had the most inventive copywriter for its July 1852 advertisement in the *Sacramento Daily Union*:

JOHNSON & COMPANY'S OPPOSITION LINE OF STAGES FROM SACRAMENTO TO SHASTA—From Sacramento by Steamboat to Colusa—Thence by splendid four horse coaches to Shasta. Passengers by this route can have a good night's rest on the steamer, and not be subjected to the tedious and uncomfortable stage traveling in the night. The road from Colusa is mostly upon the banks of the Sacramento River, and shaded by large oak trees, which gives this route a decided advantage over other conveyances.

Twelve miles south of Red Bluff, Tehama City (part of Colusa County until 1856) was a principal ferry crossing over the Sacramento River between Marysville and Shasta and an important center where stagelines converged, creating lively and prosperous activity until the railroad came north in the 1870s. Today, Tehama is a quiet community surrounded by orchards.

Shasta grew to be the largest town in Shasta County, a thriving supply center of 3,500 residents serving upward of 15,000 miners in neighboring Trinity County and the upland mining districts that became part of Siskiyou County in 1852. Over time, scores of stage drivers wheeled into town; 145 drivers' names are immortalized on two identical bronze plaques erected by Mae Helene Boggs in 1931 to honor her uncle Williamson Lyncoya Smith, Shasta County's most famous stageman.

Smith was twenty when he rode into Placerville in August 1850, a gold seeker who followed other young men to the Reading Diggings and on to the Trinity River region. He quit mining to become a packer, loading freight on the backs of horses and mules for the trip over the Siskiyou Mountains into Oregon, later

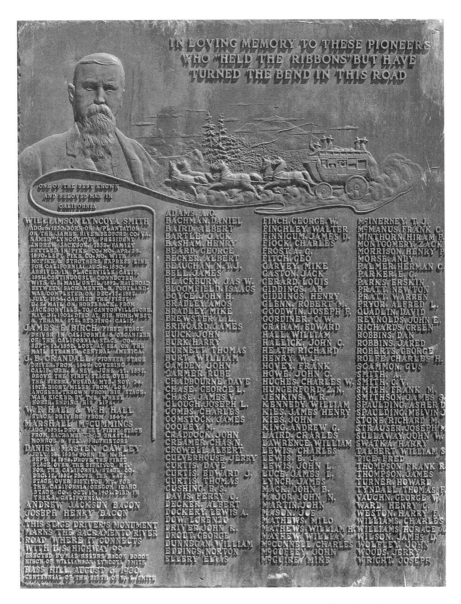

Detail of the Stage Driver's Memorial plaque, listing 145 names. *Photo by author.*

signing on as a stage driver for the California Stage Company. Smith drove the first daily mail and passenger stage on the California–Oregon Stage Road over Scott Mountain in 1860, when the California–Oregon Stage Company began operating its line from Sacramento to Portland. He was appointed its division road superintendent between Shasta and Jacksonville, Oregon, a post he held until he retired from staging. Williamson Lyncoya Smith died at his home in Redding on May 31, 1902.

The flourishing gold-mining towns of Weaverville and Yreka were among the last in upper northern California to receive stage service. Stagemen Warren and William Hall and their equally resourceful partner J.B. Crandall established a line between Marysville and Yreka in 1853 but found that they could go no farther with a stage road than twenty miles above present-day Redding at French Gulch. Forced to resort to mule trains to convey both mail and passengers beyond that point, they blazed a semicircular trail northwestward. Three years later, the California Stage Company hacked out another semicircular route oriented northeastward, judged a terrible road by all who suffered a three-day stagecoach journey from Red Bluff. The company had no time to improve it, as Indian hostilities forced its closure after two months.

A wagon road connecting Shasta and Weaverville opened in October 1857, considered fine enough for a buggy to travel with ease. The first stage into Weaverville made its appearance at five o'clock in the afternoon on Thursday, April 29, 1858. The California Stage Company coach was escorted into town by a number of citizens in buggies and on horseback and the German Brass

The gold mine at Long Gulch, near Yreka, sketched by Daniel A. Jenks in 1860. *Library of Congress, Prints & Photographs Division.*

Band. Finally, in September 1860, the combined efforts of the Shasta and Yreka Turnpike Company and the California Stage Company succeeded in completing a decent stage road from Shasta to Yreka.

Weaverville and Yreka continue to flourish. Shasta City began depopulating after the Central Pacific Railroad bypassed it in 1872 to create the town of Redding, named for the railroad's land agent and former Sacramento mayor and California secretary of state Benjamin B. Redding instead of Major Pierson Reading (the two names are pronounced the same), as Shasta County residents would have preferred. Today, the town site is a state historic park containing several restored 1850s-era buildings and the half ruins of others.

DUTCH FLAT AND THE DUTCH FLAT & DONNER LAKE WAGON ROAD

Today a registered California Historical Landmark community along Interstate 80 with fewer than two hundred residents, Dutch Flat once boasted a population of two thousand. It is not and never was on flat land, nor was it established by Dutch settlers—facts that elicited querulous comments even in the nineteenth century. In 1851, Prussian immigrants Joseph and Charles Dornbach and their families settled on a grassy forest clearing along the emigrant trail. The Germans, or Deutsch, were called "Dutch" in that era's common slang, and a meadow-like clearing within an alpine forest was sometimes known as a "flat." Although probably not the Dornbachs' preference, the name stuck.

Their settlement was in the midst of a mining region that encompassed Green Valley, Little York and Mountain Springs or Cold Springs (later known as Gold Run). All of these camps were supplied by pack-mule train from Illinoistown (today's Colfax), the head of stagecoach and wagon navigation for several years because, in less than fifteen miles east, land elevation sharply ascended another thousand feet. However, in 1853, a Mr. T.H. Brigham ran a stage service between Dutch Flat and Illinoistown, and in 1857, the Dutch Flat Stage Company established daily stage service between the two towns over Madden & Company's toll road, connecting with other lines emanating from Illinoistown to Auburn, Grass Valley and Sacramento. Passengers boarded and disembarked the stage at the well-appointed, three-story Dutch Flat Hotel or at the National Hotel across the street.

Main Street in Dutch Flat, 1860s. *Library of Congress, Lawrence & Houseworth Collection.*

Beginning in 1854, Dutch Flat enjoyed a thirty-plus-year gold-producing heyday achieved from hydraulic mining techniques and a flourishing lumber business from 1861 into the opening years of the next century. Massive migration eastward to Nevada's fabulous Comstock Lode began in the summer of 1858, migration that initially used the Placerville–Carson Valley and Henness Pass routes. January 1863 marked the ceremonial inauguration of the Central Pacific Railroad (CPRR), and Dutch Flat became an important stage stop when the builders of the CPRR chose it as the starting point for a wagon toll road into Nevada to both capture revenues from Comstock traffic and to facilitate the transport of materials and workers as the rails progressed. Opened in June 1864, the Dutch Flat & Donner Lake Wagon Road (DFDLWR) skirted the north side of Donner Lake before veering off near today's Stampede Reservoir to connect with the Henness Pass Road. Wide enough to permit vehicles going in opposite directions to easily pass one another, and with grades never exceeding ten inches to the

Polley's Station at Crystal Lake. Henry Polley was a superintendent during construction of the Dutch Flat & Donner Lake Wagon Road. *Library of Congress, Lawrence & Houseworth Collection.*

rod going east, the densely traveled DFDLWR was touted by its builders as "the shortest, best and most comfortable road."

The California Stage Company commenced running its coaches over the DFDLWR on July 16, 1854. Stagecoaches stopped at Pollard's Station, a village at Donner Lake containing J.D. Pollard's two-story hotel, a blacksmith shop and a general store. After Pollard's Hotel twice succumbed to fire, residents relocated to a new settlement called Coburn's Station, a stage station and public house selected as a camp for the railroad's construction crews. Coburn's Station was renamed Truckee in April 1868.

Dutch Flat lost much of its importance as a stage stop when the CPRR reached Cisco twenty miles farther up the ridge in 1866, and stage companies removed their operations headquarters to the new railhead. In 1913, the DFDLWR route over the Sierra was chosen as a segment of the new coast-to-coast Lincoln Highway for automobile traffic. Portions of the Lincoln Highway alignment became U.S. Route 40 in 1928.

EPILOGUE

By January 1890, phrases such as "The old days of the stagecoach" and "That now comparatively unknown vehicle, the stagecoach" were frequently appearing in various publications, mainly referring to the trans-Sierra stage routes that had been eliminated by the iron horse. The Central Pacific Railroad had long since crossed the Sierra Nevada for points east, supplanting the stagecoaches that once crowded the Placerville, Dutch Flat and Henness Pass Roads. Now, a network of rail lines crisscrossed the bay area and extended down the coast. Within the previous twenty years, the Central Pacific and its subsidiaries, successors and competitors had spread through the central valleys south into Los Angeles and north into Oregon, creating new communities and depopulating others as they progressed. Metropolitan-area newspapers no longer published stage routes and schedules, and few staging concerns were awarded mail contracts from the end of that decade forward.

In December 1887, "An Enchanted Editor," writing for the *Salt Lake Tribune*, sang the praises of the railroad, copied by the *Sacramento Daily Union* in its December 27 issue:

> *Tomorrow the men of California and Oregon will celebrate the completion of a work of more magnitude than many people dream of. The road between San Francisco and Portland is at last completed, and the Southern Pacific Company now own a line continuous from the Columbia River to San Diego. The men who, in forty years, have attacked and subdued that*

land…have a right to rejoice that at last they are joined together with a band of steel, and that they are at last made independent of ship and stagecoach.

Nevertheless, multiple stage lines were still operating in 1890 as the primary means of transportation beyond the reach of the rails. The heyday of the California stagecoach was past, but in 1890, its final run was still twenty years in the future. Before the end of the 1880s, the gasoline-powered "auto-mobile," perfected by Gottlieb Daimler and Karl Benz, was generating considerable interest, although some years would elapse before sufficient infrastructure was in place to inspire confidence in motoring long distances. The automobile slowly usurped the stagecoach in fits and starts, in most cases typical of the evolutionary process that occurred in Amador County.

The Southern Pacific reached Ione in 1876, hailed as a vast improvement over the "abominable" stage road from Galt, but as 1900 dawned, John Raggio still operated his family's ten mail and passenger coaches daily over six lines through Amador and Calaveras Counties. Having become involved in banking, he sold his stage lines to Fred Raab of Sutter Creek in 1904, a few months before the Ione & Eastern Railroad built a spur from Ione to a terminus at Martell, two miles from Jackson. John Steiner, who owned the stage line between Jackson and Plymouth, added another vehicle to connect with the El Dorado stage to Placerville in 1903. In 1910, C.L. Miller started a new "much-needed" stage line (as the *Amador Ledger* opined) between Jackson and Plymouth, a three-and-a-half-hour trip, including stops at intersecting towns. A year later, Miller announced he would cease operations for lack of patronage but resumed service within three months when travel increased again in the spring. During this decade, the Globe and National Hotels were Jackson's stage depots.

Two new horse-driven stage lines opened during this period, but change was coming with the advent of Frank Atterberry's auto stage service between Jackson and Sacramento in the summer of 1909. Atterberry and his one automobile were not particularly successful, but the following April, the owner of the local garage made another attempt. Thorp's auto stage line ran between Jackson and Ione on roads reported as fairly good, if somewhat rough in places.

In October 1909, the *San Francisco Call* declared, a bit prematurely for all northern California locales, that the auto stage had succeeded the traditional stagecoach: "The automobile stage has succeeded the coach and six, and the old time mule skinner now swaps lies with his colleagues about the peculiar antics of a carburetor instead of those of the off leader."

Jackson's National Hotel advertisement dated 1911—after decades, still the proud stage office for all points. *Author's collection.*

In December 1911, a group of capitalists established an auto stage line departing Jackson's National Hotel for Plymouth, with plans to extend service to all the towns of Amador County's mineral belt. Their auto stages were sixty-horsepower Ramblers capable of carrying sixteen passengers, connected with other cars at Plymouth for Sacramento, and made two round trips daily.

Meanwhile, Amador City residents were traveling by stagecoach to various destinations, and a crowd of young people enjoyed a ride to Jackson in a private automobile—all in the same week. The four-horse stagecoach from Fiddletown (then known as Oleta) bound for Plumas County in December 1911 and filled with fifteen passengers had a driver whose hair, garments and demeanor were those of a man "imitating a period of the stage in its pristine glory long since passed into the shades of pioneer days," or so said one passenger.

This plaque marks the 1850s site of John Mohler Studebaker's wagon repair shop. *Photo by author.*

That unnamed Fiddletown stage driver was one of a diehard breed who wanted no other occupation and probably resented the evidence of inevitable change pressing in around him: horse-less carriages and those Wright brothers' flying contraption demonstration at someplace called Kitty Hawk. Instead, it was the forward-looking aspirations of others from those same old pioneer days that spelled the demise of the stagecoach. The men who built the Central Pacific Railroad had been gold rushers, as was John Mohler Studebaker, a co-founder of the Studebaker Corporation automobile company.

The lure of California's gold brought nineteen-year-old John to Placerville in August 1853, traveling overland in a wagon he had helped his brothers build. After three months of lackluster mining, he opened a shop on Main Street, where he sharpened miners' picks, repaired wagons and landed a contract to manufacture wheelbarrows. John returned to his brothers' blacksmith shop in South Bend, Indiana, in 1858, investing his accumulated savings in the family's fledgling wagon-making business. Studebaker Wagon Factory (which did not manufacture stagecoaches) became known across America for quality wagons and carriages.

EPILOGUE

The Studebaker brothers entered the automobile market with an electric car in 1902, followed by a gasoline-powered vehicle in 1904. Dozens of other entrepreneurs jumped on the automobile-manufacturing bandwagon, including Cadillac, Oldsmobile, Packard, Ford and Hudson. Automobile sales reached record heights in 1909 (with Los Angeles leading in California) and were expected to quadruple the following year. Motorcar enthusiasts formed clubs, arranged group outings and sent emissaries to the state capital to demand the construction of paved highways. Fifteen-seater, motorized tourist hotel buses and the larger double-decker motorbuses already prevalent in London and New York were not far behind in reaching California.

Placerville gave eighty-year-old John Mohler Studebaker a royal welcome when he visited in April 1912, a time when enough gas pumps and mechanics' shops already lined the state highways to enable Studebaker and his party to drive a company-manufactured motorcar from San Diego to San Francisco. Placerville resident T.R. Stevens, who had owned the stage line from Placerville to Shingle Springs back in 1872, housed one of his best old Concord coaches on his property—and reported that his grandchildren used it as a playhouse. Sacramento, once the stagecoach capital of the nation, paraded an old coach drawn by six horses through the city's business section for the 1912 State Fair's Pioneer Day.

The end of a glorious era. *Author's collection.*

EPILOGUE

From the early 1880s through 1913, *Buffalo Bill's Wild West Show* glamorized the stagecoach with audience-thrilling melodramatic skits of dashing drivers eluding masked highwaymen and Indian arrows. The new motion picture industry followed suit, exaggerating gunplay by fantastic outlaws engaged in fierce attack as white-hatted heroes prevailed, also disregarding the stagecoach's true function as a valuable system of transport and communication. In the summer of 1913, mountain resorts such as Skaggs' Hot Springs in Sonoma, Campbell Hot Springs in Sierraville, Lake Independence fifteen miles from Truckee, Yosemite Valley and Shasta Castle Crags informed their patrons of regular stagecoach service from rail stations to their lodges *and* the on-site availability of oil and gasoline for private automobiles.

One day in the 1920s—no one can quite put a definitive finger on it—the magnificent Concord, with its expert driver manipulating the reins of a four or six in hand, just wasn't there anymore. The lament published by Nevada's *Virginia Chronicle* in 1874, a mere five years after the completion of the first transcontinental railroad destroyed staging activity on the trans-Sierra roads, still resounds as a fitting tribute to the glory days of California stagecoaching:

The Old Stage Lines. A farmer appeared in town this morning with a load of chickens in a stagecoach which once belonged to the famous Pioneer Stage Company. The upper work had been cut out from the middle and the center of the vehicle was filled up with poultry coops, and the ranchman handled four horses from the seat perhaps once occupied by Hank Monk or some other noted driver, who used to swing his team of six blooded horses around the turns on the Placerville route within an inch of yearning precipices, never meeting with an accident and always getting through on time. To such base uses we come at last.

Who...can forget the keen relish with which he who was fortunate enough to get a seat on the top beside the driver enjoyed the ride over the mountains...the climb up steep ascents; the joy with which he sped through forests of mighty pines...and drew up in front of [a town hotel] covered with dust, amid the crowd of people who always assembled to see the stage come in.

BIBLIOGRAPHY

Amador County Chamber of Commerce, 2013.

Angel, Myron. *History of Placer County, California*. Oakland, CA: Thompson & West, 1882.

Architectural and Historic Resources of Auburn, California. National Register of Historic Places. National Park Service, United States Department of the Interior, 2002.

Banning, Captain William, and George Hugh. *Six Horses*. New York: Century Company, 1930.

Burnett, Peter H. *Recollections and Opinions of an Old Pioneer*. New York: D. Appleton, 1880. [Retrieved from California Digital Library E-Book and Texts Archive, May 8, 2013.]

California Genealogy & History Archives. San Joaquin County Biographies, John Raggio.

Chandler, Dr. Robert. "California Stagecoaching: The Dusty Reality." *Dogtown Territorial Quarterly* 47 (2001).

———. "Wells Fargo: A California Company Goes North of the Border." *California Territorial Quarterly* 58 (2004).

———. "Wells Fargo Never Forgets." *California Territorial Quarterly* 78 (2009).

———. "Wells Fargo's Stagecoaching, an 1860s Turf War." *California Territorial Quarterly* 69 (2007).

Daily Picayune. "Ship Passengers for California." January 2, 1849. [Downloaded from sfgenealogy.com, June 16, 2013.]

BIBLIOGRAPHY

Dogtown Territorial Quarterly 5 (1991). [Reprinting the *Chico Daily Record*, June 26, 1864.]

Fourteenth Anniversary of the Society of California Pioneers, Oration by Rev. Henry W. Bellows, September 9, 1864. San Francisco: Alta California Book and Job Office, 1864.

Fradkin, Phillip L. *Stagecoach Book One: Wells Fargo and the American West.* New York: Simon & Schuster, 2002.

Gallucci, Mary McLennon, and Lieutenant Colonel Alfred D. Gallucci. *James E. Birch.* San Francisco: Sacramento County Historical Society, 1958.

Kibbey, Mead B., ed. Facsimile reproduction of *J. Horace Culver's Sacramento City Directory for the Year 1851.* Sacramento: California State Library Foundation, 2000.

———. Facsimile reproduction of *Samuel Colville's Sacramento City Directory for the Year 1853–54.* Sacramento: California State Library Foundation, 1997.

Kyle, Douglas E., ed. *Historic Spots in California.* 5th ed. Palo Alto, CA: Stanford University Press, 2002.

Marschner, Janice. *California 1850: A Snapshot in Time.* Sacramento, CA: Coleman Ranch Press, 2000.

Maryland Historical Society. Summary of McLane-Fisher Family Papers, ca. 1800–1905. [Available online.]

Mason, Jesse D. *History of Amador County, California.* Oakland, CA: Thompson & West, 1881.

Moody, Ralph. *Stagecoach West.* Lincoln: University of Nebraska Press Bison Books, 1998.

Nottingham, Mary E. "A Remarkable Man." Swansea Historical Society: Roots Web Genealogy. [Downloaded April 13, 2013.]

Parker, Marilyn. *The Pollock Pines Epic.* Placerville, CA: Placerville Press, 1988.

Placer County Archives and Collection Center, Auburn, California. Various primary materials re: the Mountaineer House and Jack Phillips.

Secrest, William B. *Perilous Trails, Dangerous Men: Early California Stagecoach Robbers and Their Desperate Careers, 1856–1900.* Clovis, CA: Quill Driver Books/Word Dancer Press, 2002.

Shasta Stage Drivers' Monument, Shasta SHP, California.

Smith, Dottie. "Redding vs. Reading." *Dogtown Territorial Quarterly* 13 (Spring 1993).

Special Census in California. Santa Clara County, July 21, 1852.

Stone, Irving. *Men to Match My Mountains.* Garden City, NY: Doubleday & Company, 1956.

Thompson and West. *History of Yuba County, California*. Oakland, CA, 1879.

Tinkham, George H. *History of San Joaquin County, California*. Los Angeles: Historic Record Company, 1923.

Traywick, Ben T. "Missing Treasure on Trinity Mountain." *Tombstone News*, May 27, 2013.

United States Census, June 1870. Santa Clara Township.

United States Congressional Serial Set. Issue 2854, p. 601.

Vineyard, Ron. "Stage Waggons and Coaches." Colonial Williamsburg Foundation Library Research Report Series. Williamsburg, VA, 2002.

West, Ron. "Hazards of Stage and Express." *Dogtown Territorial Quarterly* 9 (Spring 1992).

Wilson, Neill C. *Treasure Express*. Glorieta, NM: Rio Grande Press, Inc., 1987.

Newspapers

Alta California

Amador Ledger

California Farmer

The Elevator (San Francisco)

Los Angeles Star

Marysville Daily Herald

Pacific Rural Press

Placer Herald

Placer Times

Sacramento Transcript

Sacramento Union

San Francisco Call

Sausalito News

INDEX

INDEX

ABOUT THE AUTHOR

Cheryl Anne Stapp is the author of the award-winning *Disaster & Triumph: Sacramento Women, Gold Rush Through the Civil War* and *Sacramento Chronicles: A Golden Past*. She lives with her husband in Sacramento—in bygone days, an important gold rush town and the largest staging center in the nation. To learn more about California history, visit her website, "California's Olden Golden Days," at http://cherylannestapp.com.

Visit us at
www.historypress.net

....

This title is also available as an e-book